FACES OF
TIME

75 YEARS OF TIME MAGAZINE COVER PORTRAITS

FACES OF TIME

75 YEARS OF TIME MAGAZINE COVER PORTRAITS

Introduction by **Jay Leno**   Essay by **Frederick S. Voss**

A Bulfinch Press Book

in association with the
National Portrait Gallery, Smithsonian Institution

Little, Brown and Company
Boston · New York · Toronto · London

This book was published on the occasion of the exhibition "Faces of TIME: 75 Years of TIME Cover Portraits" at the National Portrait Gallery, Smithsonian Institution, Washington, D.C., March 20–August 2, 1998. Subsequent exhibition venues are: National Academy Museum, New York City; Chicago Historical Society, Illinois; Edsel and Eleanor Ford House, Grosse Pointe Shores, Michigan.

First Edition

ISBN 0-8212-2498-0
Library of Congress Catalog Card Number 97-77748

Designed by Rudolph Hoglund

Bulfinch Press is an imprint and trademark of Little, Brown and Company (Inc.)
Published simultaneously in Canada by Little, Brown & Company (Canada) Limited

PRINTED IN SINGAPORE

CONTENTS

FOREWORD

Henry Muller

ACKNOWLEDGMENTS

Frederick S. Voss

WILL I BE ON THE COVER IN NEW JERSEY?

Jay Leno

BEING ON TIME: THE EVOLUTION OF A TRADITION

Frederick S. Voss

PLATES

CHECKLIST OF THE EXHIBITION

Foreword

THE MOST EAGERLY AWAITED EVENT IN THE EDITORIAL CYCLE AT TIME IS ALWAYS the selection of the cover. Late in the week, usually on Friday night, editors and art directors converge in a conference room to argue the relative importance of major stories, to opine on the artistic and journalistic merits of various images, and finally to hone the cover billings that, one prays, will make the next issue irresistible to readers. Even when the choice of subject matter is easy—who can argue against, say, putting the President-elect on the cover after his victory?—there may be animated debates over which words and image best capture the moment. When there is either no news or too much news, the discussions can go on for hours and the decision can be excruciatingly difficult.

If passions run strong, it is because the cover embodies what TIME is all about: editorial judgment you can trust, clarity and conciseness of expression, aesthetic sensibility—and of course a commercial imperative. Magazines, after all, are sold. So when the debate is over and the managing editor has ruled, the hope is that one has reconciled what sometimes seems irreconcilable. The best covers capture the zeitgeist of the week while surviving the judgment of history. They carry an image that inspires readers to grab the magazine off the newsstand while being worthy of someday being included in a book like this.

Journalism, as the old saying goes, is the first draft of history. What is amazing, as one delves into this volume, is how often the editors got it right. One could do worse than review seventy-five years of TIME covers to recall the events, ideas, and emotions that have defined what the magazine's co-founder, Henry Luce, called the American century. From the beginning, Luce and his fellow editors believed that many stories can best be told through people. Thus cover portraiture became a natural extension of TIME's journalism. As thematic stories became more common, editors and artists rose to the challenge with some of the innovative visual approaches you'll see in this book. The result is that even today, in the age of omnipresent television, networked computers, and screaming tabloid headlines, TIME's words and art collaborate to provide the perspective that brings millions of readers back every week.

One regret I occasionally felt while choosing covers during my years as managing editor of TIME was that two-dimensional representation on a relatively small, red-framed, disposable surface did not always capture the full richness of the works that were delivered to our offices—for example, a globe wrapped by Christo or a delicate lacquered box bearing a portrait of Gorbachev. We are grateful to the National Portrait Gallery for having organized a traveling exhibit that will, in this year of TIME's seventy-fifth birthday, allow many Americans to enjoy the magazine's cover art firsthand just as we editors do. We also thank them for participating in the production of this companion volume, which extends the life of these many remarkable unions of journalism and art beyond the seven days for which they were originally intended.

Henry Muller
Editorial Director, Time Inc.

Acknowledgments

T O IDENTIFY THE FIRST CAUSE FOR THIS PUBLICATION AND THE EXHIBITION it accompanies, it is necessary to go back to 1978. That year, TIME magazine presented the National Portrait Gallery with some eight hundred pieces of original artwork commissioned for its covers. In the two decades since, TIME has added to that collection with a number of other such gifts. Today the gallery's TIME Collection includes just over eighteen hundred objects. Because the bulk of these pieces are portraits of prominent twentieth-century newsmakers, the gallery counts the TIME Collection among its prized assets, and the first order of business on this occasion is to express once again the museum's profound gratitude to TIME for entrusting it with the magazine's cover legacy. Warm thanks also are due TIME for the funding of this current enterprise and for its many forms of nonfinancial support and encouragement.

Much gratitude is owing as well to many individuals who provided invaluable assistance in enlarging my understanding of the cover tradition. Among them are Helcia Chaliapin, widow of cover artist Boris Chaliapin, and June Williams, granddaughter of cover artist Ernest Hamlin Baker, both of whom made available clippings and correspondence related to TIME covermaking. Also of enormous help was Linda Warner Constantino, who so willingly shared with me the results of her own investigation into the more contemporary trends in TIME covers. As for Bill Hooper of the Time Inc. Archives, I am eternally grateful for his ever prompt efforts to fill my research requests. Finally, no words can fully express my appreciation to retired cover researcher Rosemary Frank, who is a font of information on covers past and perhaps the most loyal friend that the TIME Collection will ever have.

Among my colleagues at the National Portrait Gallery, I am especially grateful to photographers Rolland White and Marianne Gurley, who supplied many of the reproductions for this book. Also indispensable to this undertaking have been the museum's exhibit designers, Nello Marconi and Al Elkins, and conservators Cindy Lou Ockershausen, Rosemary Fallon, and Emily Klayman. Last, but by no means least, I offer sincerest thanks to Curator of Exhibitions Beverly Cox for her central role in coordinating both the exhibition and this book and for all the moral support she has given me on this and many previous occasions.

Frederick S. Voss
Historian and Curator for the TIME *Collection*
National Portrait Gallery
Smithsonian Institution

WILL I BE ON THE COVER IN NEW JERSEY?

By Jay Leno

On March 16, 1992, I was on the cover of TIME. When they called to let me know about the decision, I immediately thought of Mort Sahl. I had always been a big fan of Mort, and I knew that he had once been the cover story. That image really made an impression on me because he was the first comedian I could remember being featured on the cover of TIME.

When I called my Mom back in Boston to tell her the news, she said, "Now TIME, which one is that? Is that the one like *People?*"

I explained to her that TIME was the one with "Man of the Year."

She said, "Oh, you mean the red one."

I told her to make sure and call Aunt Fay in New Jersey and all my uncles and cousins in New York, to put them on alert so they could get copies. She said, "You won't be on the magazine down there. They'll only put you on the cover up here because this is your hometown. Somebody else will be on the ones they sell in New Jersey."

I have to admit, before the issue actually arrived, there was a fear factor. It's called "getting bumped." If it happens in comedy clubs and on late-night talk shows, it must happen in the magazine business. TIME has all these plans to put me on the cover, everything is going smoothly, the issue is ready to go to print, a war breaks out somewhere in a country I can't spell or pronounce, and all of a sudden, I'm a sidebar on page 74. Which would have just vindicated my Mom's insistence that each town has a different cover.

When the issue finally came out, my first reaction was selfish. I kept thinking how unfair this was to happen to me at the age of forty-two instead of when I was nineteen. Because being on the cover of TIME just has to be a great way to meet girls. "Would you like to come to my apartment and see the sketch Al Hirschfeld did of me on the cover of TIME?" That's clearly one of the all-time great pickup lines. It certainly beats, "Hi, I'm a sophomore at Emerson, what's your major?"

I remember reading a description, some twenty or twenty-five years ago, of a dinner party TIME had where all the guests were people featured on the cover. How fantastic would it be to attend something like that? If you just take the subjects featured in the National Portrait Gallery's exhibition *Faces of* TIME, the guest list at that dinner party would include eight presidents, five top military leaders, two popes, Churchill, Einstein, and the Beatles.

For better or worse, the cover defines you in popular culture. Because in the information age, in an era when people are bombarded on a daily basis with thousands of facts, figures, and fleeting images, the TIME cover gives 23 million subscribers and countless others a common reference point. For seventy-five years, Americans have talked about, and comedians have poked fun at, the person on the cover. My monologues tend to center on it for one simple reason: a comedian needs no other setup for a joke than to say, "Did you see this week's TIME magazine?" In a diverse culture, the cover is a universally recognized shorthand.

I once heard it said that television is like skywriting. It's there, you see it, and then it's gone. It's true for the viewer—and is also true for the host. I loved doing show number 1299 tonight, and the minute the lights go down, I move on to show number 1300.

Which is one reason being on TIME has been so important to me. That cover, solid in its framed, glossy permanence, is an important milestone in my life. No matter what happens to me in show business, it is something that, ten, twenty, thirty years from now, I can look back upon. Being on the cover is the single most amazing thing to ever happen to me.

Jay Leno by Al Hirschfeld
TIME, March 16, 1992

TIME

Jay
LENO

**Taking over
the throne
after Carson's
remarkable
30-year reign**

Everything is going smoothly, the issue is ready to go to print, a war breaks out somewhere in a country I can't spell or pronounce, and all of a sudden, I'm a sidebar on page 74.

TIME founders Briton Hadden and Henry Luce, with Cleveland city manager William R. Hopkins, examining the August 31, 1925, issue.

BEING ON TIME: THE EVOLUTION OF A TRADITION

By Frederick S. Voss

N FEBRUARY 1922 CUB REPORTERS BRITON Hadden and Henry Robinson Luce quit the *Baltimore News* after only three months on the job and headed for New York City. No idle whim, this relocation had been on their agenda ever since the summer of 1918 when, having just completed their sophomore year at Yale, Hadden and Luce spent the summer in an army training camp in South Carolina preparing to join the American Expeditionary Force in Europe. To their disappointment, the war ended before they could make it to the battlefields of France, and they returned to Yale. But their military experience had borne fruit: while in camp,

Hadden and Luce, who had worked closely together on school newspapers at Hotchkiss preparatory school as well as Yale, began to talk about founding their own news publication.

By the time they were settled in a dingy makeshift office on Manhattan's East 17th Street, the nature of this publishing venture was pretty well defined: they would establish a weekly magazine that reduced a week's news into short, easily digestible articles so that readers might stay informed without expending a great deal of time and effort. The pair was certain this sort of periodical would find a profitable niche in the news business. They were also convinced that it could not help but promote the democratic ideal of a well-informed populace.

Hadden and Luce's enthusiasm for their enterprise, soon christened TIME, was not widely shared. When they set out to raise $100,000 to

Fig. 1

William Oberhardt. Retiring congressman "Uncle Joe" Cannon. TIME, March 3, 1923

FIFTEEN CENTS

TIME

The Weekly News-Magazine

VOL. 1, NO. 1   MARCH 3, 1923 start the magazine, they encountered many a polite brush-off. But by October 1922 they had raised some $86,000, and they decided to launch the magazine. In late November TIME was incorporated, and they had begun to assemble a small staff. The following February the first issue, dated March 3, 1923, rolled off the press.

Somehow the magazine made it through its first year, with an average circulation of 18,500 for the second half of 1923. At the end of 1924, circulation stood at 70,000, and by 1930 it reached 300,000. Fast becoming one of the country's major journalistic institutions, it eventually would be one of the most influential news publications in the world.

One ingredient of the magazine's success was a distinctive journalistic style that had considerable popular appeal. Its chief component was crisp, zestful, sometimes irreverent writing that featured colorful descriptive phrases, neol-

ogisms, and words drawn from relatively obscure corners of the dictionary. Terms such as "omnivendorous," coined to describe the ever-broadening scope of American drugstore merchandising, or "eel-hipped runagade," applied to football star Red Grange, irked TIME's more tradition-minded readers, and the magazine's application of such unflattering adjectives as "paunchy," "unkempt," and "gimlet-eyed" to public figures struck many as cheap shots.[1] On the other hand, TIME's prose had its admirers, and within a few years of its founding, the magazine's writing was being imitated. By the early 1930s, seasoned editors and publishers, including the British newspaper mogul Lord Beaverbrook, were putting TIME on "must read" lists for their staffs.

Also contributing to TIME's success was its decision to report the news with heavy emphasis on the personalities who shaped it. The most obvious evidence of TIME's preoccupation with personality was its cover. The maiden issue of TIME bore a reproduction of a charcoal drawing of the octogenarian former Speaker of the House Joseph G. Cannon, who was retiring from Congress after serving forty-six years *(fig. 1)*. The story that accompanied this image did not fill even a column, but the cover portrait set the pattern for one of the magazine's most predictable features: for many years to come, TIME's cover would generally bear the likeness of a newsworthy individual.

There were exceptions; in February 1928, in tandem with a story on show dogs, a young basset hound graced the cover. In the fall of that year, as the presidential contest between Al Smith and Herbert Hoover came down to the wire, the cover featured a photograph of a crowd over the caption "The People." But such exceptions only underscored the rule. Throughout most of its history, images of newsmakers—presidents, generals, foreign potentates, movie stars, and poets—have been the primary staple of TIME's weekly covers. Even in more recent years, although the magazine has gravitated increasingly to issue-oriented covers, the newsmaker likeness is still the subject matter most readily associated with its cover tradition.

Fig. 2

Unidentified photographer. Alphonse "Scarface" Capone. TIME, March 24, 1930

Woods recalled that being a cover subject was a pleasantly exciting experience until he reported for duty to a battle-scarred company captain in occupied Japan.

As TIME grew and prospered, its newsmaker cover portraits took on ever greater interest and significance in the public mind. It is not known just when it first struck TIME readers that the magazine's covers were collectible, but by the 1950s removing a cover and sending it to the cover's subject to be autographed had become a hobby of individuals around the world. Chief among the cover hounds was retired U.S. Army colonel Robert F. Carter, who by 1963 possessed 1,100 autographed covers, which represented more than half the issues TIME had published to that point. When British prime minister Harold Wilson made his first appearance on a TIME cover in 1963, he was flabbergasted by the huge numbers of covers sent to him for signing. Forewarned was forearmed, and when he sat for his second cover portrait two years later, he urged the artist to leave an open space for autographing in the lower portion of the likeness.[2]

Another indication of popular interest was the strong reader reaction that some of the covers engendered. When a dapper Al Capone in a silk necktie smiled out from the magazine's cover in 1930, readers were outraged that the magazine should feature on its cover the country's most notorious criminal *(fig. 2)*. The occasion was Capone's release from a Pennsylvania prison after ten months of incarceration for unlawfully bearing arms. One reader called it "an insult to every subscriber and an outrage to public decency"; another charged the magazine with insulting all its other cover subjects by placing an image of this "depraved miscreant of the lowest type" in the featured spot; yet another remarked that "everybody knows that TIME is published in Chicago," insinuating that the magazine must be under Capone's thumb.[3]

There is no record of how Al Capone felt

about being on a TIME cover. If he was like the other cover subjects, however, he most likely was flattered. For the more the magazine grew and prospered, the more an appearance on its cover became the measure of greatness. On May 13, 1945, for example, a German general in full dress uniform walked into a U.S. Army command post to give himself up. When he was brought before an American general for preliminary interviewing, he identified himself as "General Nikolaus von Falkenhorst, the former commander of all the German land, sea and air forces in Norway." Then, as if to make sure that everyone properly grasped his importance, he added, "Your famous TIME magazine had my picture on the front page, and they described me as the master of land, sea and air." In the movie *A Woman of Distinction,* the stature of Rosalind Russell's character is underscored by her appearance on a TIME cover. Russell hung the fake cover in a lounge near her pool, and she was not above letting visitors think it was for real, until, several years later, she actually did appear on the cover.

In at least one instance, making the cover of TIME was not only a source of considerable satisfaction for the cover subject himself; it was as well the cause for a kind of national celebration. When Australia's prime minister Robert G. Menzies rated a cover in 1960, his countrymen seemed to regard it as the next best thing to a Second Coming in Melbourne. As the Menzies issue quickly sold out at newsstands and vendors clamored for more, many Australians took

Fig. 3 (above)
Ernest Hamlin Baker. West Point's Woods, First Captain. TIME, June 11, 1945

Fig. 4
Paul Dorsey.
Walter Winchell.
TIME, July 11, 1938

Fig. 5
Paul Dorsey. Mr. Rodgers and Mr. Hart. TIME,
September 26, 1938

it all as a sign that their country was finally achieving the weightier status that it deserved in the international community.

While being the subject of a TIME cover story is often good for the ego, there can be a downside, as Robert Woods learned in the fall of 1945. The recent West Point graduate had been featured on the cover the previous June in tandem with a story on West Point. Woods recalled that being a cover subject was a pleasantly exciting experience until he reported for duty to a battle-scarred company captain in occupied Japan. After exchanging salutes with Woods and verifying that he was talking to *the* Robert Woods of TIME cover fame, the captain launched into a story of some particularly grueling combat he and his men had endured the previous June in the Philippines. Just as the fighting ended, he said, a mail orderly brought him a copy of the issue of TIME bearing Woods's likeness *(fig. 3)*. The thought that TIME was holding up the untested Woods as an emblem of America's soldiering capabilities while seasoned fighters such as himself sat unheralded in a Pacific jungle was too much to bear. At that moment, said the captain, he swore that if he ever ran into West Point Group first captain Woods in the flesh, he would shoot him. With that, he pulled from his desk a .45-caliber revolver and grimly pointed it at Woods. Fifty years or so later, Woods could not remember just how he managed to escape unscathed. On one point, however, he had no doubt: the captain was in earnest, and for a few tense

moments Woods thought that he was about to die, the victim of TIME cover fame. The next day the captain, clearly suffering from battle fatigue, was sent home.[4]

In the magazine's early years, TIME's newsmaker covers generally alternated between charcoal drawings and black-and-white photographs. The photos, supplied by agencies, were usually undistinguished. More noteworthy were the charcoal likenesses, drawn by various artists, which in composition and expression were apt to be lively and eye-catching. The one of Joe Cannon that ran on the cover of TIME's maiden issue was the work of illustrator William Oberhardt, who made the drawing in the fall of 1921 and was convinced by Hadden and Luce to license it to them for onetime publication. Many years later, Oberhardt recalled that the sitting for the picture took place in Cannon's Capitol office and that as Oberhardt drew, the crusty Cannon received visitors and periodically availed himself of the room's several cuspidors. Upon finishing the portrait, Oberhardt asked to sketch a second one, hoping to capture a better likeness. The impatient Cannon walked across the room to have a look. "You don't want to do that again," he declared, "that's homely enough."[5]

For the second issue of TIME, Oberhardt provided a likeness of President Warren G. Harding. That was his last work for the new magazine, however, and over the next year and a half or so an artist named Gordon Stevenson was the principal source for its charcoal cover portraits. Little is known about Stevenson or his working relationship with TIME, but a good deal is known about the artist who succeeded him. He was Samuel J. Woolf, a native New Yorker who had trained at the Art Students League. With his considerable talent, Woolf might well have enjoyed success as a painter of studio portraits. But even as a young man hungry for clients, he bristled at the requirement of most portrait commissions that likenesses be done to the satisfaction of sitters. And that, Woolf lamented, all too often meant that the artist had to sacrifice his own perception of his subjects in favor of "painting people as they thought they looked."[6] Finally, after serving as a frontline artist-correspondent for *Collier's* during World War I and experiencing considerable success as a lithographer, Woolf hit upon a way to pursue portraiture on terms suitable to himself: in the early 1920s he began drawing likenesses of literary figures for the book section of the *New York Times,* and in 1923 he started to produce charcoal portraits of current notables for the *Times* Sunday magazine and features sections.

Woolf supplied his first cover for TIME (a likeness of Pope Pius XI) in June 1924. Recalling years later his initial impression of the new magazine's daily operations, he rated his first visit to its offices as "an experience I am unlikely to forget." "The confusion and lack of system," he said, "exceeded anything I had ever seen."[7] But TIME managed to keep Woolf happy, and over the next several years he was generally the artist it called upon for doing its nonphotographic portrait covers. In all, he supplied the magazine with nearly two hundred likenesses, including one in oil of car magnate Walter P. Chrysler, which ran in January 1929 and was TIME's first full-color cover.

A good many of Woolf's TIME newsmaker portraits were derived from photographs. Not surprisingly, the artist did not find this especially satisfying and felt that it tended to produce "a copy instead of an interpretation."[8] Circumstances, however, sometimes permitted personal encounters with the subjects. Perhaps the early TIME cover that most authentically captures a newsmaker at his or her moment of greatest newsworthiness is Woolf's likeness of Charles A. Lindbergh, for which the young aviator posed in Paris soon after completing his historic solo transatlantic flight *(page 50).*

Viewed collectively, Woolf's TIME covers of the 1920s and 1930s tend to blend into one another because nearly all of them were done in charcoal and their head-and-shoulders compositions are often similar. Yet some of them are remarkably vibrant, such as the 1933 likeness of labor leader John L. Lewis, which is invested with a flesh-and-blood immediacy, conveying the subject's bull-like presence and volatility *(page 52).*

TIME was calling on Woolf for his services less and less by the mid-1930s and instead moving toward the greater use of photographs on its covers. By 1938, thanks to advances in printing technology, these photographic portraits were generally in full color. That year produced some of the most animated cover likenesses yet seen on TIME, including one of Broadway columnist Walter Winchell speaking on the telephone in a *Front Page* pose, and another of songwriting team Richard Rodgers and Lorenz Hart at work on a composition *(figs. 4 and 5).*

Behind this move toward more dynamic covers was Dana Tasker, who came to TIME in December 1937 from *Newsweek (fig. 6).* Tasker was hired to be editor of TIME's Business and Finance section but was soon assigned to reorganize the picture department, which led to his taking charge of the covers. A horse-racing en-

There were a good many . . . readers . . . who did not at all mind having a little sexiness mixed in with their weekly news regimen.

Fig. 6
Dana Tasker. Photograph by Roy Stevens

thusiast, Tasker definitely had a risk-taking temperament. One of the best evidences of that was the full-length cover likeness he commissioned in 1941 showing movie star Rita Hayworth in all her leggy glory *(fig. 7)*. The work of famed pinup artist George Petty, the chiffon-clad image was a marked departure from TIME's generally sedate head-and-shoulders treatment. So it probably came as no surprise when it generated unusually strong responses from readers—both pro and con. A Minnesota college professor quickly dashed off a telegram: "SHAME ON TIME FOR DISTINGUISHING PETTY'S INDECENT VULGAR DISTORTIONS OF FEMALE FORM. . . . LET SUCH CRUDENESS STAY IN ADVERTISING WORLD WHERE SANE PEOPLE CAN IGNORE IT." No less indignant was a Mrs. Ford of Philadelphia: "Do you think that the majority of your subscribers will not be offended by the frontispiece on TIME . . . displaying the almost nude body of Rita Hayworth? If you do, I think that you fail to sense the desire of many intelligent readers of TIME to stand for a high stan-

dard of morals." There were a good many other readers, however, who did not at all mind having a little sexiness mixed in with their weekly news regimen. While one Robert Shinbaum registered his enthusiasm for the Hayworth cover with a "WOW!" Emil Erickson and Paul Cundy expressed their approval with a "WOW!!!" and Paul Zimmerman voiced his with a "WOW!!!!!!!!"[9]

Tasker's commissioning of Hayworth's controversial likeness was of minor note, however, compared to his pivotal role in formulating a type of news portrait that was for decades as integral to TIME's newsstand identity as its title logo. Sporadically foreshadowed in 1938 and 1939, the image consisted of a meticulously realistic painted likeness complemented by backgrounds and symbols alluding to the reason for the subject's newsworthiness. By late 1941, just as the nation was girding itself for entry into World War II, this brand of newsmaker portraiture was entrenched as TIME's prevailing cover style.

To develop the new formula, Tasker found an ally in commercial artist Ernest Hamlin Baker. At Colgate University, where he had been a track star, Baker had defrayed some of his college expenses by selling caricatures. By the late 1930s he had managed to build quite a good reputation as an illustrator. TIME's publisher Ralph Ingersoll had, during his tenure at *Fortune*, been so impressed with Baker's work that he was convinced that the artist could "do anything."[10] When Tasker indicated his wish to explore new cover styles, Ingersoll told him to try Baker.

Baker did his first cover for TIME in February 1939, a two-tone likeness of the Polish musician-statesman Ignace Jan Paderewski, and it

Fig. 7
George Petty. Rita Hayworth.
TIME, November 10, 1941

TIME

THE WEEKLY NEWSMAGAZINE

RITA HAYWORTH

Fred Astaire has a new partner.

(Cinema)

VOLUME XXXVIII   (REG. U. S. PAT. OFF.)   NUMBER 19

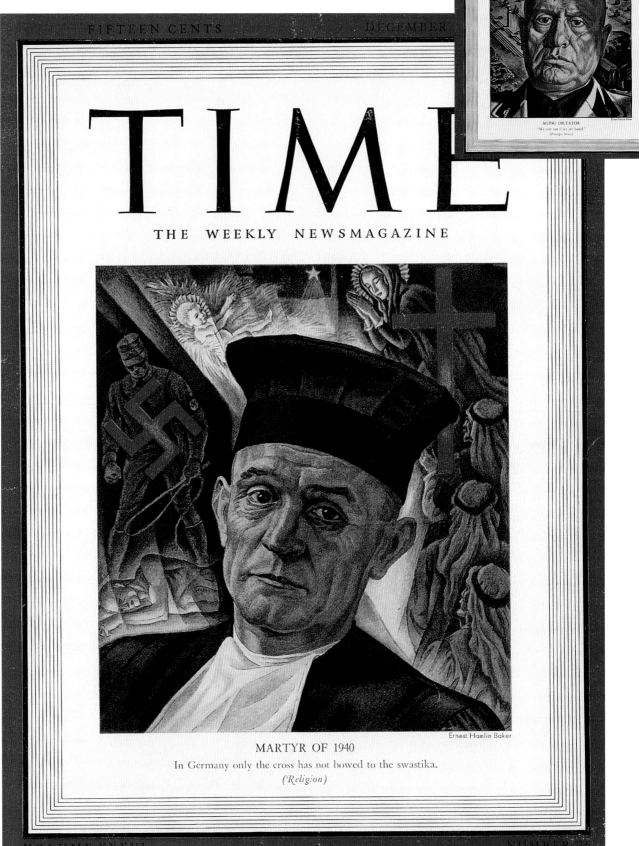

FIFTEEN CENTS   DECEMBER

TIME
THE WEEKLY NEWSMAGAZINE

MARTYR OF 1940
In Germany only the cross has not bowed to the swastika.
(Religion)

Ernest Hamlin Baker

VOLUME XXXVI   (REG. U. S. PAT. OFF.)   NUMBER 26 required two nearly sleepless days to complete. Not long afterward TIME asked him to do a cover portrait of newspaper mogul William Randolph Hearst. Exceptionally strong in its rendering of the aging and financially troubled Hearst, the likeness drew plaudits from a reader who could not decide whether he thought the insight of the cover or of the article it accompanied represented "the greater triumph."[11]

Baker's first newsmaker images were all set against plain backgrounds. But in late 1940, he and Tasker began to conceptualize a cover portrait that provided readers with a shorthand and somewhat subliminal explanation of its news context, and in December Baker produced a cover image of German Lutheran pastor Martin Niemöller that exemplified their ideas. Flanked by a cross and a swastika meant to suggest his and other German Christian clerics' opposition to the Nazi regime, the likeness became the template for hundreds of covers to come (fig. 8).

Baker's time-consuming method began with spending hours scrutinizing photographs of the subject with a magnifying glass and then advanced to making a preliminary drawing, which Baker called a "facial map," that delineated the features in minute detail. He slowly built up the final painting with thin washes of color. The result was a crisp image that occasionally seemed brutal in its factuality. One reader complained that although he held "no brief for Mussolini," he found Baker's treatment of him totally disgusting (fig. 9).[12]

Baker supplied over half of TIME's covers in 1941, including the one of Henry Ford seen here (fig. 10), and by the time he retired in 1956, the magazine had published nearly three hundred of his portraits. Under ideal circumstances, Baker's laborious process required ten or twelve days, and by the spring of 1941, the effort to keep TIME supplied with covers was wearing him down. Most tiring of all were probably those portraits that, owing to some late-breaking news, were asked for with little advance notice. One of the artists brought in to relieve Baker was the Russian-born Boris Artzybasheff, who did his first cover (of Chinese general Chen Cheng) in June 1941 and re-

mained a regular cover artist for the magazine until his death in 1965. A descendant of the Polish patriot Thaddeus Kosciusko through his father, Russian novelist-playwright Mikhail Artzybasheff, the artist was in his late teens when his country was torn by revolution. In the midst of ever-shifting chaos, he found himself drafted into a German-backed Ukrainian army, but rather than serve, he followed his father's advice to get out of Russia. Slipping through the lines of both the White and Red armies using the identification papers of another man, he eventually made his way to the Crimea, where he became a deckhand on a Black Sea steamer. In the spring of 1919, the ship set out for the United States with a cargo whose sale was intended to raise money for replenishing the arms of the flagging White faction. Shortly after the boat docked in Brooklyn in June 1919, he decided to jump ship, and with just a few cents' worth of Turkish currency in his pocket, Artzybasheff went in search of a means to support himself in the New World.[13]

Although he had trained to be a lawyer, his passion had always been drawing, and he found

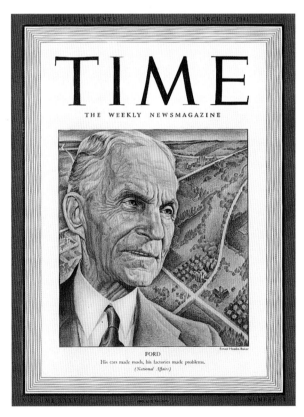

Fig. 10
Ernest Hamlin Baker. Henry Ford. TIME, March 17, 1941

his first job at an engraving firm. With his rimless pince-nez glasses and neat mustache, Artzybasheff looked "for all the world like a cautious banker."[14] But the pin-striped exterior housed a whimsical mind, and among his specialties were fantastic book and magazine illustrations that transformed the modern technology of machinery and weapons into recognizable human forms. His early TIME covers did not look all that different from Baker's, but he increasingly gave them unique twists, and although Tasker and others at TIME worked out cover concepts with artists beforehand, Artzybasheff's realization of a concept was often "worlds away" from what was expected.[15]

Striking early examples of this unpredictable originality are his 1943 cover renderings of German grand admiral Karl Doenitz and Japanese admiral Osami Nagano *(pages 54–55)*. While a more conventional artist might have portrayed Doenitz, the brain behind Germany's deadly U-boat strategy, against a watery background and with a submarine on the horizon, Artzybasheff transformed Doenitz into a periscope-like projection of one of his own vessels. In Nagano's likeness, he expressed his flair for unusual imagery by setting Japan's director of naval strategies on the deck of a battleship anthropomorphized into a gun-toting Western outlaw.

Like Baker, Artzybasheff was a painstaking craftsman who preferred a generous lead time for the completion of his covers. In a note he made on one of his last covers for TIME, a likeness of Laotian general Kong Le, he disgustedly remarked, "Painted with every kind of muck . . . will look lousy in reproduction. [But] what the hell can you expect in four days?"[16]

Artzybasheff could thus alleviate the pressure on Baker only partially. The final antidote for that problem did not come until the summer of 1942 in the form of another Russian-born artist, Boris Chaliapin. As ebullient and expansively gregarious as Artzybasheff was buttoned-up, Chaliapin was the son of Feodor Chaliapin, regarded by some as the finest opera bass ever. Like Artzybasheff, he too lived through the Russian Revolution. His family initially held hopes for the Communist regime, and with his father proclaimed a "people's

artist," Chaliapin remained in Russia to complete his art training. Officials in the newly established Soviet system of art education placed him in a program for would-be sculptors when he really wanted to be a painter. For a while he tolerated this indifference to his personal preferences, but finally he decided to pursue his artistic ambitions elsewhere. In 1925 he emigrated to Paris with the help of his father, whose own disillusion with the Soviet regime had led him to settle there as well. Chaliapin's staunch adherence to realism, however, made him uneasy with avant-garde trends prevailing in the Paris art world, and in 1935 he moved to New York City in hopes of finding a climate more in tune with his conservative view of painting.

Tasker first heard about Chaliapin in mid-1942 through Laird S. Goldsborough, a former editor of the magazine's Foreign News section, who met Chaliapin through their mutual interest in opera. After a personal interview, Tasker was impressed enough to commission the artist to do a cover of Jawaharlal Nehru, one of India's leaders in its struggle for independence. The result was a strikingly shadowed portrayal, which Chaliapin justifiably numbered among his best pieces for TIME *(fig. 11)*.

Although TIME was sufficiently impressed with his *Nehru* to want Chaliapin to do other covers, the magazine's editors did not initially know of his amazing facility for quick draftsmanship, which was destined to give him a very special niche on the magazine's roster of cover artists. Perfected in timed drawing exercises at a school in Paris, that talent did not remain hidden for long. A few weeks after the Nehru portrait appeared, unexpected events in the British battle to block the German drive into Egypt prompted the magazine to ask him for a last-minute cover portrait of General Sir Harold Alexander. Told that the piece had to be at the publisher in less than twenty-four hours, Chaliapin began the likeness in the evening, soon after he agreed to do it, and early the next morning it was ready for delivery. His reputation for speed was firmly established at TIME, and he became the artist to whom the magazine turned for its quick cover fixes. Sometimes that distinction annoyed Chaliapin and caused him incon-

TIME

THE WEEKLY (NEWSMAGAZINE

INDIA'S NEHRU
When do the British go? When do the Japs come?
(Foreign News)

Boris Chaliapin

Fig. 11
Boris Chaliapin. India's
Nehru (Jawaharlal Nehru).
TIME, August 24, 1942

venience. But he had himself largely to blame, because as the years passed, he only became faster. Eventually he could complete one of TIME's rush requests in as little as seven hours.

Artzybasheff, Baker, and Chaliapin were soon known around the magazine as the "ABCs" *(fig. 12)*. While Baker continued to supply covers for seventeen years, Artzybasheff went on doing them for twenty-four and Chaliapin for twenty-eight. Between 1939, when Baker handed over to TIME the first of the trio's

newsmaker portraits, and 1970, when Chaliapin completed the last of them, the ABCs executed some nine hundred covers, which represented well over half those published in that thirty-one-year period. But longevity of affiliation and number of covers tell only half the story, and "triumvirate" may be more appropriate than mere "trio" to describe their place among TIME cover artists. For although the three artists had their stylistic differences, their covers adhered pretty much to the same formula, and in doing

so, they set the stylistic rules and standards for many years to come for most of the other artists who were brought into TIME's stable.

Although TIME had clearly defined by 1941 the overall look of its cover portraiture, it doesn't follow that the week-in-week-out production of covers during World War II boiled down to a routine matter. To the contrary, wartime covermaking was often fraught with difficulties. To begin with, the magazine did not always have the most accurate information regarding the enemy. Consequently, when TIME settled on a cover story focused on some aspect of Axis operations, the decision about which enemy leader was most appropriate to feature on the cover was sometimes a matter of educated guesswork.

The magazine's feature story for the issue of September 21, 1942, was the German army's progress in its drive to control southern Russia and to take the strategic city of Stalingrad. To complement the story, TIME's cover for that issue carried an Artzybasheff rendering of the cadaverous features of German field marshal Fedor von Bock, who, according to the magazine's sources, was commanding the drive. Of Germany's generals, Bock ranked among the

most ruthlessly indifferent to the safety of his men. His nickname was "der Sterber" (angel of death), and he never tired of telling his men that their ultimate glory was "death in battle."[17] But, interesting as all this was, Bock should not have been a part of this cover story. In early July he and Hitler had had a falling-out over Bock's deployment of tank forces, and by the time the September cover story ran, Bock had long since been relieved of his command and returned to Germany.

Late-breaking news from the battlefronts often necessitated last-minute cover changes. In late April of 1945 the magazine had decided that the cover for its May 7 issue would feature Marshal Georgi Zhukov, the man leading the Soviet army's push toward Berlin. Just as the Zhukov cover was rolling off the press, news broke that something had happened to Hitler. TIME could not determine whether he had committed suicide, been executed, or was merely under arrest. But two things were certain: the man whose territorial ambitions had set Europe aflame was done for, and the magazine faced a last-minute cover change. Fortunately, TIME had built up a store of potential cover portraits to meet such emergencies. Staffers came up

The man whose territorial ambitions had set Europe aflame was done for, and the magazine faced a last-minute cover change.

with a portrait of Hitler by Artzybasheff and sent it to the printers with instructions to superimpose a large red X on Hitler's face *(fig. 13)*. The scrapped cover stock amounted on this occasion to some fifteen tons.

But the Hitler-for-Zhukov switch was small potatoes compared to what the magazine had gone through to arrive at its cover for November 16, 1942. At first it appeared that the biggest news of the week was the progress by American and Australian forces in the Solomon Islands, so Australia's prime minister John Curtin was to be on the cover. Within a day or so, the Solomons story was overshadowed by Republican gains in off-year elections, and Curtin was dropped in favor of New York's newly elected GOP governor, Thomas E. Dewey. No sooner were the Dewey covers coming off the press than a third cover seemed in order as Allied naval successes in the eastern Mediterranean were reported, and so eight hundred thousand Dewey covers went into the waste bins as TIME staffers scurried around for a likeness of Great Britain's rear admiral Sir Henry Harwood. But the fickleness of wartime news had yet to run its course. As the Harwood cover was being printed, word came that American forces, under the command of General Dwight D. Eisenhower, were landing in North Africa. As a result, when TIME finally hit the newsstands, its cover bore the likeness of Eisenhower.

There was at least one happy moment during the war when TIME managed to gain the upper hand in foreseeing what its next cover should be. In late July or early August 1942, when military censorship was keeping a tight lid on news of any big moves against Japanese strongholds in the Pacific, the magazine's South Pacific reporter, John Hersey, learned that a massive operation was about to be launched against the Japanese at Guadalcanal in the Solomon Islands. He could not tell his editors in New York unless he wanted to lose his press credentials, but he did succeed in getting a

Fig. 13
Boris Artzybasheff. Adolf Hitler.
TIME, May 7, 1945

telegram through censorship stating something to the effect that "if you are *wise men* [emphasis added], you will know where one of your upcoming cover stories will be coming from."[18] Hersey hoped that readers of this message would sense its hidden meaning, and they did. Making the connection between the Bible's wise King Solomon and the Solomon Islands, they now knew the "where" for their next cover story, and from that they could deduce the Allied leader most likely to be an appropriate subject for their next newsmaker portrait. When news of the invasion of Guadalcanal reached the States shortly after it began on August 7, 1942, TIME was ready with its cover portrait of Vice Admiral Robert L. Ghormley, the American naval officer commanding the early stages of this watershed operation.

FIFTEEN CENTS   January 4, 1937

TIME

The Weekly Newsmagazine

Dorothy Wilding

WOMAN OF THE YEAR

The Archbishop of Canterbury: "Truly this has been wonderful."
(See FOREIGN NEWS)

Volume XXIX   Number 1

An Annual Rite: Man of the Year

GENERALLY SPEAKING, NO COVER that TIME publishes is more prestigious or important than another. The one, however, that runs on the magazine's first issue of every year is an exception, and to be the subject of that image has come to represent the ultimate in newsworthiness. It is commonly known as TIME's Man of the Year cover, although the first word of that term sometimes requires alteration, and it features the man, woman, group, or thing that, in the magazine's judgment, has "for better or worse" most dominated events in the previous twelve-month period. In the world of journalism, this annual designation is unique, and it is no exaggeration to say that speculation regarding who will receive this honor has become a ritual, in news-minded quarters at least, almost as interwoven into year-end holiday customs as mistletoe or eggnog.

The Man of the Year tradition was born of necessity. In late December 1927, the customary holiday slowdown in news had left TIME staffers feeling hard-pressed for a suitable cover subject for the new year's first issue. Also weighing on the minds of some was the embarrassing oversight the previous spring when the magazine failed to feature Charles Lindbergh on its cover following his history-making transatlantic flight. A solution emerged: instead of a news personality of the week, the magazine would feature America's most talked-about aviator, and under his likeness would be the words "Man of the Year."

It took a while for the Man of the Year designation to root itself, but by late 1933 it was apparent that TIME's readership was getting into the spirit of the thing when word came from snowbound Hiram, Ohio, that its citizens were placing bets on the magazine's next Man of the Year. The local odds on Germany's new dictator, Adolf Hitler, the informant noted, stood at six to five, and on America's new president, Franklin Roosevelt, at three to two.[19] Unfortunately for the Hiram inhabitants who put their money on these two favorites, 1933's Man of the Year honors went to a considerably darker horse, Hugh Johnson, dynamic head of the New Deal's short-lived National Recovery Administration.

The following year, in response to an invitation from TIME, subscribers began mailing in their thoughts on who should receive the honor. Also becoming part of the tradition was a certain amount of Monday-morning quarterbacking following TIME's disclosure of its choice. The most significant newsmaker of 1936 was a Woman of the Year, American divorcée Wallis Simpson (fig. 14). The stylish Mrs. Simpson had captured the heart of the English monarch, Edward VIII, and countless front-page headlines as her royal suitor moved toward abdication so that he might marry her. Newsworthy as her affair with a king was, it nevertheless struck some readers that she was decidedly unworthy of TIME's title. "Phooey, Scallions, and Fishcakes on your most lousy choice of 'person of the year,'" fumed one. "For your editors a big and mighty Bronx cheer." Yet another, fixated on the fact that Mrs. Simpson had begun her romance with the king while still wed to another, declared her selection as Woman of the Year "a lousy insult to every faithful wife and mother in the U.S."[20]

Usually there is room for debate over who the next Man of the Year should be. But 1938 was an exception. The war-portending litany of Hitler's activities that year—from his annexation of Austria and the Czech Sudetenland to his buildup of German arms—made his Man of the Year designation a foregone conclusion. A number of readers, however, abhorred the thought of it, fearing that it could be interpreted as an American endorsement of Hitler. To avoid that possibility, one reader suggested that TIME leave the cover blank. Another thought that if the magazine must name the malevolent Hitler Man of the Year, then at least it could announce

Fig. 14
Dorothy Wilding. Woman of the Year (Wallis Simpson). TIME, January 4, 1937

a counterbalancing "Saint of the Year."

Aware of subscriber antipathy toward naming Hitler Man of the Year, publisher Ralph Ingersoll was determined that the magazine in no way betray the faintest hint of affinity for Hitler, and when he saw the color photograph of the German dictator slated for the cover, it struck him as far too flattering. Deeply troubled over running this image, which might as well have been chosen by Hitler's propaganda minister Joseph Goebbels, Ingersoll could talk of nothing else at a session soon afterward with his psychiatrist. Fortunately, the psychiatrist had a solution: if there was still time to substitute another picture, Ingersoll should look into the recent work of the artist Rudolph C. von Ripper.

Jailed in Germany for his caricatures satirizing the Nazis, Ripper immigrated to France, where he began working on *Écrasez l'infame*, a portfolio of allegorical etchings decrying Hitler and his oppressions. Shown at a New York gallery in the spring of 1938, one image in the series answered Ingersoll's cover problem. Titled "The Hymn of Hate," it depicted Hitler seated at a pipe organ as victims of his regime hung from a structure reminiscent of torture wheels used in the persecution of early Christians *(fig. 15)*. Looking on as the German dictator pounded out his tune of brutal oppression were members of Germany's artistocratic military elite, and through the spokes of the wheel could be seen a clerical figure, representing the endorsement some German clergy had accorded Hitler. This picture accomplished exactly what Ingersoll wanted and more: when TIME readers saw it on the cover of their first issue of 1939, no one—not even the most visually obtuse—could interpret it as favorable to Hitler.

"The Hymn of Hate" fell totally outside the bounds that TIME had set for its covers, and one Germanophile reader characterized its publication as the "lowest and foulest thing" the magazine had ever done.[21] As a seasoned journalist, Ingersoll had no difficulty shrugging off criticisms from the public at large. But he was perhaps not prepared to take the heat that came from within the TIME organization, from none other than the magazine's founder, Henry Luce, whom Ingersoll had failed to apprise of his cover choice. Luce was no admirer of Hitler, but he took issue with the picture's placement on the cover, which turned the magazine's most important pictorial feature into an editorial page—something that it had never been. Recalling his post-publication discussion of the matter with Luce, Ingersoll said that Luce was livid, and through much of the exchange his face was drained of color. "Have you any idea what you've done?" he raged. "A basic tradition destroyed . . . everything I've built . . . in one gesture." Then Luce calmed down, and there was silence. After a moment, he said, "Spilt milk."[22] The interview was over. Although the incident was never mentioned again, it certainly did not help the already difficult relationship between the two, which ended shortly after

MAN OF 1938
From the unholy organist, a hymn of hate.
(Foreign News)

Rudolph Charles von Ripper

Fig. 15

Rudolph Charles von Ripper. The Hymn of Hate. 1938. TIME, January 2, 1939

when Ingersoll left TIME to found his own newspaper.

Luce's no-editorial cover policy, however, was not quite as absolute as his reaction to the Hitler image suggested. As long as the editorializing was reasonably subtle, it was all right. At least that was the implication of Ernest Baker's cover rendering twelve months later of 1939 Man of the Year, Soviet dictator Joseph Stalin (fig. 16). Owing his Man of the Year title to his unexpected alliance with Hitler just weeks before the outbreak of World War II, Stalin was not exactly reduced to an out-and-out villain by Baker. Still, the likeness's grinning, demonic swagger was no neutral commentary. That became especially clear three years later when Stalin again became Man of the Year, this time as the fighting ally of the United States (fig. 17). On that occasion, TIME cast Stalin in an unmistakably heroic mold. As one reader wryly put it, the "satanic" Stalin of three years back seemed to have graduated into the ranks of the "Christlike."[23]

Because the Man of the Year choice is not linked to the latest news developments and, by its nature, claims transcendent importance, it is quite unlikely that any eleventh-hour news could be so earth-shattering as to force TIME to trade in one Man of the Year for another, but this happened in 1941. By early December, with much of the globe already embroiled in World War II and American involvement in that conflict becoming ever more direct, the magazine had decided that the conversion of the country's industries to armaments production had been the most significant story of the year. For its next Man of the Year, TIME had therefore settled on car manufacturer Henry Ford, who had led the way in much of the conversion. A cover portrait of Ford—his visage framed by gently curving rows of military tanks and warplanes—was in hand.

But then came the Japanese attack on Pearl Harbor on December 7 and the declaration of war. Suddenly the choice of Ford as Man of the Year seemed trivial, and the editors decided that Ford would be bumped in favor of President Franklin Roosevelt, who now faced the awesome task of leading the nation safely through global war.

The magazine turned to Ernest Hamlin Baker. Although his slow working methods did not lend themselves to rush jobs, the artist accepted the commission, and doubtless there were moments over the next several days that made him sorry that he had. The short lead time did not permit Baker to conduct, as was his wont, color experiments before settling on the piece's final color scheme, which was to be done in muted tones of red, white, and blue. Then there was the fact that the magazine had asked for the inclusion of background likenesses of the leaders of America's two new wartime allies, Winston Churchill and Joseph Stalin, which of course meant that Baker was required to do three portraits instead of the usual one. But, worst of all, it was decided that, in keeping with the current crisis, Roosevelt's face had to be deadly serious, and the photograph that TIME's editor in chief insisted that Baker work from was, the artist said, "not so hot."

Despite the aggravating circumstances, Baker persevered, putting in "12 to 14 hours a day" for four days running. Finally the piece was done, and by the time it was dispatched by train to the printer in Chicago on the late afternoon of December 15, Baker actually had come to think well of his handiwork (fig. 18). Whatever its shortcomings, he later told the man who bought the original artwork from him, "I still think it is a good job of wartime portraiture." Then, however, he muted that note of satisfaction, adding, "Roosevelt has not written me about it which is perhaps just as well!!!"[24]

In 1950 Man of the Year took on a new wrinkle. Instead of going to a named individual, the title went to a generic person, the "U.S. fighting man," otherwise known as "G.I. Joe" (fig. 19). The occasion for this unexpected choice was the Korean War, which represented the first real test of this country's cold war fighting mettle. To the average civilian reader of TIME, the cover likeness by Ernest Baker, depicting a fictional G.I., doubtless seemed appropriate. But for an army combat artist named Robert Weldy Baer, who had been drawing the faces of real G.I.s in Korea, this helmeted, square-jawed image struck a false note, so much so that he was prompted to write Baker about it. At the heart of Baer's objections was the fact that Baker's handsomely gritty, self-assured soldier, who seemed to come out of Hollywood central casting, simply did not square with his own overall impressions of the faces of rank-and-file G.I.s in Korea. According to Baer, those men were considerably more boyish-looking and

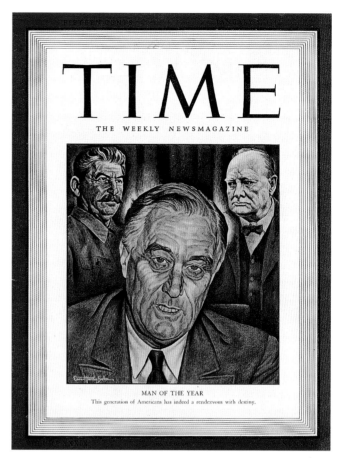

Fig. 18

Ernest Hamlin Baker. Man of the Year (Franklin D. Roosevelt). TIME, January 5, 1942

tended often to have a "bewildered" look about them, and while there may have been "strength" in their faces, there was also "no understanding" of the situation.[25]

Although it is unlikely that TIME would have accepted any attempt to diminish the soldierly dignity of its G.I. Joe, it was quite another matter when it came to the cover portrayal of the 1957 Man of the Year, Soviet leader Nikita Khrushchev. There was no doubt that Khrushchev's extraordinary string of accomplishments that year entitled him to that designation. In addition to putting Soviet agriculture and industry on new and possibly more productive footing, he had established warmer ties with China, acquired important new friends for his country in the strategically crucial Middle East, and halted the growing disaffection for the Soviet Union among its Eastern European satellites. Above all, perhaps, and certainly most galling for Americans, he had presided over the Soviet Union's triumphant launchings of

MAN OF THE YEAR
Name: American. Occupation: Fighting-man.

In the cold war's double-entry ledger, Khrushchev's triumphs were U.S. setbacks, and that made it difficult to acknowledge him with sporting grace.

Sputniks I and *II*, the first man-made satellites to orbit the earth, which had so shattered U.S. confidence in its technological superiority.

Khrushchev deserved to be Man of the Year, but in the cold war's double-entry ledger, his triumphs were U. S. setbacks, and that made it difficult to acknowledge him with sporting grace. Nowhere was that more apparent than in Khrushchev's Man of the Year cover by Boris Artzybasheff *(fig. 20)*. Only a few steps short of being a cartoon, it showed the Soviet leader topped off by a birthday-hat model of the Kremlin as he gloatingly admired his reflection in a model of *Sputnik* held in his stubby, fat hands. Clearly the intent was patronizing derision.

While the unflattering take on Khrushchev seems to have generated no objection among readers, that was certainly not the case with John F. Kennedy's 1961 Man of the Year portrait *(page 64)*, which numbers among the most fiercely maligned. The magazine had gone to considerable trouble to hire one of Europe's most prestigious portraitists, Pietro Annigoni, and then arranged for him to have sittings with his subject at the White House. The staff there were put off by the artist when he arrived tieless and wearing an old sportsman's jacket, but First Lady Jacqueline Kennedy knew of his reputation, and after she expressed approval, staff were more cooperative.

Annigoni had access to Kennedy over three days, and although he was frustrated by his subject's unwillingness to sit still for more than a few moments, he was permitted to observe and sketch Kennedy for hours at a time as he conducted the nation's business. In the process, Annigoni was privy to a soberly deliberative side of Kennedy that contrasted sharply with his smiling, youthful glamour in more public moments. In the final portrait it was this grimmer, and less frequently seen, dimension that the artist chose to emphasize.

When Annigoni brought the picture to New York for approval, Assistant Managing Editor

James Keogh worried about its grim tone and, left to his own devices, might well have opted to seek out an alternative image. When his boss, Managing Editor Otto Fuerbringer, saw the likeness, however, he was instantly taken with it and unhesitatingly decided that it should run with little modification. Some readers shared Fuerbringer's enthusiasm; one called it a "masterpiece," and another declared it "astonishingly truthful." A good many others, however, were mightily offended by its sobriety and the slightly disheveled impression created mainly by Kennedy's carelessly askew tie. "Any 'artist,'" railed one, "who can make a portrait of our president look like Quasimodo . . . should be boiled in his own oils." Another reader dismissed the likeness as "a jaundiced Dracula in ragpicker's clothing in a background of bile!"[26]

As for the two parties most directly involved in creating this cover art, the artist and his presidential model, it was perhaps no surprise that Annigoni thought well of it, while the image-sensitive Kennedy stood with the Dracula school of opinion. When asked to respond to the furor over his handiwork, Annigoni, whose gravely serious portrait of Queen Elizabeth II had several years earlier caused a similar controversy in the British Isles, staunchly stood by the truthfulness of the portrait. "I've seen the man at work and that's what I wanted to produce," he said. "I'm capable of criticizing myself. But from the point of view of interpretation, I quite agree with myself."[27] Kennedy, on the other hand, who could be extremely sensitive to the least hint of negativism about him in the press, was furious when an adviser, who had had a sneak preview of the cover, told him it was none too flattering. Without waiting to see the portrait for himself, he immediately put in a call to TIME's Washington correspondent, Hugh Sidey, ranting, "You sons of bitches have done it again."[28]

Kennedy's successor, Lyndon B. Johnson, could be every bit as prickly about unflattering

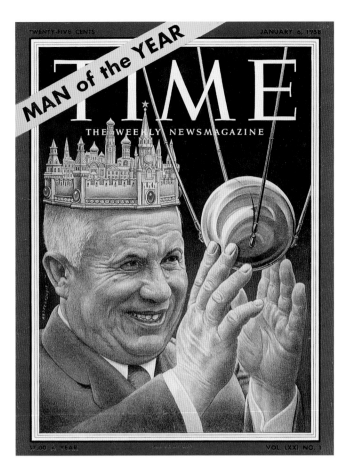

Fig. 20
Boris Artzybasheff. Man of the Year
(Nikita Khrushchev). TIME, January 6, 1958

visual images, and through much of his administration the White House went to absurd lengths to ensure that photographers shot Johnson only from his left side, which he considered his handsomest. But when TIME named him its 1964 Man of the Year, Johnson certainly could not complain about the cover portrait done to mark the occasion, and not just because it featured his left side. Based on life sketches made at the White House, the picture was the work of the well-known southwestern artist Peter Hurd, and it depicted him against a sun-drenched Texas landscape that included a rendering of his humble rural birthplace. In terms of its overall impact, it constituted a compelling blend of outdoor rusticity and presidential dignity, and although Johnson initially expressed some dismay at Hurd's treatment of his eyes, he ended up liking the portrait immensely *(page 80)*. He liked it so much, in fact, that he decided that Hurd was the artist to paint his official White House portrait. Unfor-

tunately, that commission ended in disaster with Johnson dismissing the second Hurd likeness of him with the much-publicized comment that it was "the ugliest thing" he ever saw.

In Man of the Year lore, Richard M. Nixon can lay claim to a singular distinction: seven other figures (Winston Churchill, Joseph Stalin, Dwight Eisenhower, Lyndon Johnson, Deng Xiaoping, Ronald Reagan, and Mikhail Gorbachev) have occupied the Man of the Year cover twice, and another individual (Franklin Roosevelt) appeared in that spot three times. But Nixon's fifty-seven appearances on TIME covers (Man of the Year and otherwise) will probably never be equaled, and he is the only one to be designated Man of the Year twice in succession.

The first time was in 1971, a year that witnessed any number of watershed events for his administration, from unprecedented measures to rein in the nation's mounting inflation to the first steps toward normalizing diplomatic relations with Communist China. To mark those events visually, TIME settled on one of its most unusual Man of the Year cover images, a three-dimensional papier-mâché portrait by Stanley Glaubach whose surface had been finished off with newspaper headlines underscoring Nixon's activism of the past twelve months *(page 92)*. The magazine went with this image, however, only after considering two others.

One of the alternative likenesses was by Frank Gallo, a sculptor whose mannequin-inspired and highly sexual renderings of women in epoxy and polyester resin plastics had been a sensation of the 1960s. Gallo created a likeness that looked enough like its subject. But unfortunately, there was something in the way the artist accentuated Nixon's facial creases that gave him the look of a "devil incarnate," a look clearly ill-suited to the occasion. When TIME rejected his *Nixon,* Gallo was not at all happy. It had taken him two weeks to complete this piece, which he had not initially wanted to do. When the out-of-sorts Gallo arrived home with his rejected *Nixon* in tow, one of the first things he did was climb into his car and repeatedly drive over the portrait, set down in his driveway, until it was destroyed.

Another artist TIME invited to try his hand at a Nixon cover was Joseph Bowler. Borrowing his lighting from an indistinct news photo of Nixon, Bowler produced a head-and-shoulders likeness that was warmly dignified. But apparently he had gone too far in that direction to suit the tastes of the editors at TIME. As one of them put it, Bowler's Nixon seemed so appealing that "I'd even buy a used car from that guy."[29] So the magazine went in search of a middle ground between Gallo's devil and Bowler's saint and found it in Glaubach's papier-mâché. Still, Glaubach's mummy-like image has a quality of cartoonish mockery, and given the quite positive tone of the story that it ran with, that mockery seems inappropriately gratuitous.

Perhaps TIME's cover treatment of its 1971 Man of the Year had something to do with

Fig. 21

George Segal. The Computer Moves In.
TIME, January 3, 1983

Nixon's stiff-necked style, which often made it possible to respect his achievements while laughing at him. But the likeness's tone doubtless also reflected the more general anti-establishment zeitgeist that had set in amid the turmoil of civil rights and Vietnam protests and that made expressions of cynical irreverence toward public figures a much more pervasive phenomenon.

Some readers inevitably complain about every Man of the Year choice, but the one that drew the most virulent boos and hisses has to be Iran's Ayatullah Ruhollah Khomeini. Objectively speaking, the rabidly anti-American Khomeini was an entirely logical Man of the Year choice in 1979, a year that began with his coming to power and closed with his followers holding more than fifty hostages in the American embassy in Teheran. Nevertheless, TIME knew that it was bound to offend many. To at least minimize that eventuality, the publisher's letter in the magazine's 1979 Man of the Year issue took pains to remind readers that being named Man of the Year was simply a recognition of newsworthiness and not a reward for doing good. Such sweet reason, however, was clearly ignored by many readers, and in the onslaught of indignant letters that poured into TIME, the choice of Khomeini was characterized as, among other things, "appalling and disgusting," "treason," and a "slap in the face to every American citizen." One reader predicted that the followers of "madman" Khomeini would use his Man of the Year cover as evidence that he was "winning his war of wills with the American people."[30] Even in official Washington, where one might expect more sophistication, former TIME editor in chief Hedley Donovan, then serving in the Jimmy Carter administration, found himself taking "considerable heat around the White House."[31] Among his assailants was deputy CIA director Frank Carlucci, who bearded him in the Situation Room and wondered how he could explain the choice of Khomeini to his children.

Although the choice of Khomeini drew criticism, it was hard to find fault with the portrait of him *(page 99)*. The image by Brad Holland is inescapably malevolent, and for sheer impact it

easily ranks among the strongest TIME covers. Initially the magazine suggested that he try doing a waist-length portrait; it also told him, in keeping with how most covers were laid out, to leave space above his subject's turbaned head for the TIME logo and the Man of the Year headline. Though very much a maverick, he accepted the compositional guidelines, and when he took his finished waist-length image into the magazine, the editors told him they would go with it.

But Holland was dissatisfied. Telling TIME that there were a few minor alterations he wanted to make, he took the painting back to his studio, where the more he looked at it, "the more it looked like a bad art fair painting."[32] Finally he found a solution: without stopping to think how his clients at TIME might feel, he cut down his original picture until only a tightly cropped image of Khomeini's face remained. As Holland recalled, when magazine staffers saw the result, they were heartily irritated that an artist should make such a drastic change without consultation. But it quickly became clear that Holland had dramatically accentuated Khomeini's demonic expression and, in the process, invested the cover with a pervasive sense of malevolence.

The 1980s and 1990s saw the addition of some new variables in the Man of the Year tra-

Fig. 22

Christo on Long Island beach arranging *Wrapped Globe, 1988* (page 119) to be photographed, December 1987. Photographed by Gianfranco Gorgoni.

dition, the most significant of which occurred in 1982. In its search for the most important newsmaker that year, TIME cast its lot for the first time with an inanimate object. Under the headline "Machine of the Year," the magazine announced that 1982's most important shaper of events had been the computer. Yet another variation occurred in 1988, when TIME dubbed "Endangered Earth" the "Planet of the Year," in recognition of that year's disturbing rash of ecological disasters *(page 119)*.

Inevitably, such departures from the norm invited a resort to unusual cover imagery, and for the Machine of the Year cover, a foldout was created to display sculptor George Segal's life-size tableau of a couple seated in a computer-equipped living room *(fig. 21)*. To do the cover for Planet of the Year, TIME enlisted the conceptual artist Christo, who created a polyethylene-wrapped globe that he then photographed against a Long Island beach sunrise *(fig. 22)*.

But even some of the more conventional Man of the Year designees received unusual cover treatments. George Bush's 1990 Man of the Year portrait was the work of freelance photographer Gregory Heisler *(page 122)*. He took his cue from the basic premise of TIME's Man of the Year story on Bush, which held that there were two distinct sides to his presidential personality, one leading to considerable success in foreign policy and the other to a rather dismal performance on the domestic front. Heisler's response was a double exposure of Bush from two different angles.

Bringing off a picture of that sort was an iffy proposition. As Heisler put it, "one boo-boo, and his ear winds up in the middle of his face."[33] To head off such a disaster, he spent some twenty-five hours practicing his double-exposure technique with a stand-in. The rehearsal paid off. Bush's two images were as seamlessly melded as they could be in such a photograph.

TIME was pleased with this bit of camera virtuosity, seeing it as the perfect pictorial complement to its story. At the White House, reaction was not so positive. Resenting the story's half-good/half-bad take on Bush to begin with, presidential staffers thought the photograph just added insult to injury, for it was possible to interpret the Janus-like picture as an effort to brand Bush as some sort of hypocrite. Although TIME did not intend to convey that, some readers did see it that way. Most egregious of all for Bush loyalists, Heisler and the magazine had unsportingly made Bush himself a party to this gibe by prevailing on him to pose for it.

Just how offended the White House was on this last point became clear several months later, when the *Los Angeles Times* asked Bush's press office if Heisler could come in to shoot a portrait of the president for its Sunday magazine. The answer from press secretary Marlin Fitzwater was a quick and firm "no," followed by the remark, "I don't trust him." Asked about it, Heisler defended his double-exposure likeness, calling it "a complex, engaging portrait that pays homage while raising questions."[34]

CHANGING FACES

IN EARLY 1953, DANA TASKER, THE MAN most responsible for shaping the look of TIME's newsmaker covers during the previous fifteen years, resigned as executive editor. The person in charge of covers became the magazine's assistant managing editor, Otto Fuerbringer. In his early forties, Fuerbringer was no hot-blooded Young Turk eager for drastic change in the covers, but he didn't simply follow the path charted by Tasker. Whereas Tasker had often hammered out the cover concept in long conferences with the artist, Fuerbringer was more laid-back. After discussing in general terms the slant of the cover story, he was happy to let the artist work out the final conception on his own. Just how much this loosening of the reins affected the final product is difficult to measure, but it seemed to yield images that were more dynamic and unified in overall design. Among the clearest examples is Artzybasheff's rendering of Ernest Hemingway from late 1954, where the bearded visage of the Nobel Prize winner seems almost fused to a darting marlin, placed there as a reminder of Hemingway's much-acclaimed *The Old Man and the Sea (fig. 23)*.

Another innovation from the early years of Fuerbringer's cover regime was the shift from newsmaker portraits discretely separated by white space from the TIME logo to a format where the logo was superimposed on the image. As Fuerbringer recalls, this was something that some cover artists had been urging for quite a while, and it had been tried sporadically during Tasker's last year with the magazine. But it was not until 1953–1954 that it became the norm. The result was a substantially stronger overall impact.

By the end of his second year of overseeing covers, Fuerbringer had concluded that maybe a little more stylistic variety was in order, and in 1955 he began searching for potential artists able to supply it. Among the first of his discoveries was Aaron Bohrod, a Wisconsin-based painter whose trompe l'oeil still lifes suggested the possibility of an interesting new variation on the newsmaker cover formula. In May 1955 Bohrod debuted as a TIME cover-maker with a richly detailed still life depicting a snapshot of California governor Goodwin Knight pinned to a wooden board on which also were attached an array of items associated with his state's past and present. Several months later Bohrod supplied the magazine with a similar treatment of Frank Sinatra *(fig. 24)*.

One reader thought that the Knight cover was "more appropriate for a seed catalogue" than a dignified newsweekly.[35] But the fault-finding with Bohrod was mild compared to how some readers responded to Fuerbringer's enlistment of Ben Shahn to do a cover of French writer André Malraux in July 1955. Shahn's distinctive brand of social realism was quite unlike the journalistic realism found in a Baker or Chaliapin cover, and while some readers registered approval for this new note of modernism, others were not so enthralled. One reader, in fact, declared the Malraux "the ugliest picture ever shown on a TIME cover." Fuerbringer, however, was too confident in his own aesthetic judgment to be deterred from exploring new avenues in cover portraiture.

In addition to being open to broader stylistic variety in covers, Fuerbringer also took an interest in recruiting artists wanting to do their newsmaker portraits from life sittings. Going to the trouble of arranging for sittings did not necessarily guarantee a superior likeness. Nevertheless, being able to say that a portrait was drawn from life gave it a cachet of authenticity, and beginning in the mid-1950s, cover likenesses from life sittings became fairly common.

The artist most frequently called upon to do these portraits from life was the Austrian-born Henry Koerner, who insisted from the outset that he would accept TIME's cover commissions only if the magazine could guarantee a first-hand encounter with the subject. As a youth, Koerner had attended the Graphic Academy of Applied Art in Vienna, where he had studied lettering and design. After immigrating to the United States and a stint working in the poster division of the Office of War Information during World War II, he began teaching himself to

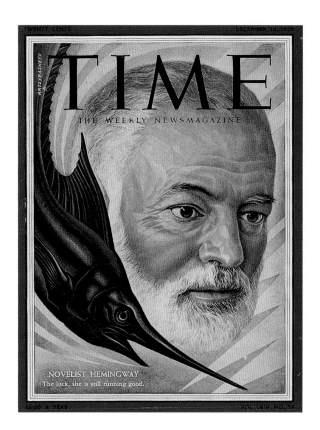

Fig. 23
Boris Artzybasheff. Novelist Hemingway (Ernest Hemingway). TIME, December 13, 1954

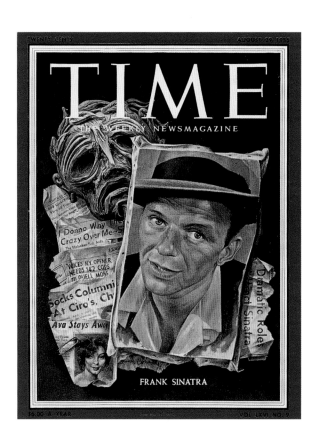

Fig. 24
Aaron Bohrod. Frank Sinatra.
TIME, August 29, 1955

On the magazine cover:

TWENTY-FIVE CENTS   JULY 29, 1957

TIME

THE WEEKLY NEWSMAGAZINE

Robert Vickrey

ACTRESS KIM NOVAK

$6.00 A YEAR   VOL. LXX NO. 5

Fig. 25
Robert Vickrey. Kim Novak. TIME, July 29, 1957

Koerner eventually produced forty-one covers over a period of twelve years. Among them were pieces that represented TIME's newsmaker portrait tradition at its best.

For Koerner, the fact that TIME honored his insistence on painting his cover subjects from life was a mixed blessing. Speaking of the prospect of doing a cover for the magazine, he once mused, "What a pleasurable dream to pose a [baseball] pitcher on the mound [Robin Roberts], a theologian confronted with Adam's skull [Paul Tillich], or a conductor in Carnegie Hall [Leonard Bernstein]!" But, when all arrangements for the sittings were made and the moment came to set brush to canvas, everything changed. As Koerner put it, that was when "pleasure stops and the fight begins." Reliving his feelings about painting Leonard Bernstein in 1957, the artist elaborated: "There he is—Leonard Bernstein, arms propped on two microphones, exhausted from rehearsing, irritated by the clicking of the clock, haunted by schedules. There I am, harassed by changes, worn down by waiting, frustrated by clumsiness and inadequacy."[37]

A memorable variant on the pleasure of anticipation and the pain of execution occurred in August 1956, when Koerner went to Italy to do a portrait of the tempestuous diva Maria Callas, who was to debut at the Metropolitan Opera in the fall *(page 60)*. Koerner arrived in Venice, where he knew Callas was vacationing, and wasted no time seeking his subject out in a cabana on the Lido. Callas informed Koerner, through her husband, that sittings must wait until she returned to Milan from her holiday.

In Milan the initial interview went well enough. Although the diva looked forbiddingly severe in a black dress and treated Koerner as something of a nuisance, she was willing to facilitate the search for a remnant of some green and red brocade to serve as a portrait backdrop. She also complied with Koerner's request to sit for a quick preliminary sketch, posed in a manner suggestive of

paint. By the late 1940s, he was exhibiting in New York surrealistic paintings that commented on the destructiveness of the war in Europe and on postwar American life. Reviewing his first one-man show in 1948, *Art News* declared him "a painter to be reckoned with." Agreeing with that summation was TIME art editor Alexander Eliot, who had claimed just a while before that Koerner "stole the show" at the Whitney Museum's Annual Exhibition of Contemporary American Painting with a visual distillation of modern America titled *Vanity Fair*.[36]

In the early 1950s, with the ascendance of abstract expressionism, figurative art such as Koerner's began losing critical favor. But Eliot still held him in high regard, and when Otto Fuerbringer asked him to recommend studio artists who might make good covers, he mentioned Koerner. It proved a good recommendation. Working in a style that was characterized by broad brushwork and mottled color effects and that clearly owed a debt to Cézanne,

Violetta pleading with her lover in *La Traviata*.

But ultimately Callas's legendary temper surfaced. At some sittings, unexpected and mildly jarring household noises would give rise to screaming, and at one of the last, she made it all too clear that Koerner himself was getting on her nerves. But rather than do something to placate her, Koerner retaliated by making her pose longer than he had originally intended. Finally the powder ignited. Callas flew into a tantrum "that shook the house" and banished Koerner from her presence.[38] The storm passed, however. A few days later, artist and subject—both pleased with the final likeness—bid each other good-bye with a friendly kiss.

Another artist who often did covers from life was Robert Vickrey, who painted his first newsmaker portrait (of dress designer Christian Dior) early in 1957. Described once as "the world's most perfect craftsman in egg tempera painting" and known for his exquisitely patterned compositions of light and shadow, he did not insist, as Koerner did, on life sittings as a precondition for taking a cover commission.[39] The majority of his seventy-odd cover portraits for the magazine were based on photographs. But while photographs did not fidget or go temperamental on him, he saw an advantage to working from life. He confessed as well that he liked living for a few days on TIME's fairly generous expense account. So, between his taste for the good life and a professional preference, Vickrey was generally pleased whenever the magazine said they had arranged for an expenses-paid meeting with his cover subject.

Of all Vickrey's cover subjects drawn from life, Robert McNamara, secretary of defense under Presidents Kennedy and Johnson, easily took the prize for detached indifference. According to the artist, he never betrayed the slightest curiosity about the likeness that was taking shape on the other side of the easel and saw his newsmaker portrait for the first time as a published cover.

At the other end of the concern spectrum was movie star Kim Novak, who posed for Vickrey in a San Francisco hotel room in 1957. The sittings got off to a pleasant start, but at some point Novak became very upset: she had

realized that Vickrey was painting her at an angle that threatened to reveal a small irregularity in her nose, and with that she put in a call to her studio to see if the sitting could be stopped. The studio, not happy with her current contract demands, was feeling rather unsympathetic and refused to intercede. Eventually Vickrey convinced her that the flaw in her nose would not show up in the likeness, but once her anxiety was aroused, it was not to be allayed. Soon she was complaining that he was omitting the flecks of ochre around her irises and told him that her eyelashes were actually longer than he was painting them. Finally she decided that the lavender blouse she had worn through several sittings would not do, and back in his studio in New York, Vickrey eventually painted over it, replacing it with a black cowl-neck sweater more to the actress's liking *(fig. 25)*.

Another difficult subject for Vickrey was Supreme Court justice Hugo Black. By the time Vickrey painted his newsmaker portrait in 1964,

Fig. 26
Robert Vickrey. Justice Hugo Black. TIME, October 9, 1964

Black had been sitting on the Court for more than twenty-five years and had become a major factor in shaping some of that body's most important decisions. But his liberal positions troubled many Supreme Court critics, and in the hope of forcing his retirement, some of them were suggesting that at age seventy-eight he was too old to be on the Court. As a result, Black was fearful that Vickrey's likeness might confirm the charges of his decrepitude, and when the artist arrived to begin sittings, he met with a strained welcome. Things became more discomforting for the artist when the justice's wife, monitoring Vickrey's brush strokes, began letting out disapproving murmurs when she thought he was going too far in the wrinkle department. At one point she pulled out a photograph of her husband taken many years earlier and wondered if Vickrey might prefer to use it as the basis for his likeness. Vickrey ultimately produced a portrait that must have come as a relief to the justice and his protective spouse *(fig. 26)*. While Black looked his real age in the picture, there was also a sense of vitality in it that belied critics' claims that he was not up to his job.

When Otto Fuerbringer went from assistant managing editor to managing editor in 1960, he continued to be a force behind the introduction of new strains into the TIME cover tradition. Even more inclined to innovation on that front was Henry Grunwald, who succeeded Fuerbringer as managing editor in 1968, and by the early 1970s, the openness to change had transformed the cover into one of TIME's most unpredictable visual elements. For evidence of that, one has only to scan the fifty-two cover images from 1970. That twelve-month period began with a People of the Year cover titled "Middle Americans," a collage mounted on painted wood by Vin Giuliani, featuring stylized profiles of a nameless man and woman whose heads rise out of an assemblage of miniature objects connoting American middle-

class life. The period ended with a cover that carried the boxy, modernistic interpretation of an American family by the sculptor Marisol. Those two pieces bracketed a wildly varying array of covers that included an appliquéd textile evoking the heritage of the American Indian by Norman Laliberté; a photomontage of actors Henry, Jane, and Peter Fonda by Andy Warhol; an expressionistic interpretation of civil rights activist Jesse Jackson by Jacob Lawrence; and a needlepoint likeness of *Women's Wear Daily* publisher John Fairchild. TIME covers, in short, were not what they used to be.

Just when all this variety became the prevailing trait of TIME covers is hard to say. But a dramatic indication that an evolution was under way was the 1965 cover portrait of ballet dancer Rudolf Nureyev *(page 71)*. Of all the newsmaker likenesses to appear on the cover, Nureyev's was easily among the least recognizable. The work of the esteemed Australian-born painter Sidney Nolan, the image verged on the abstract, and its vaguely delineated features had little in common with the tight realism that had so long been the magazine's hallmark.

Nolan's objective was to convey the sensitivity he had perceived in Nureyev while watching him grapple with a role in rehearsal. That intention was lost on many readers, one declaring the image to be "as exciting as a dish of cold oatmeal." Others, however, thought it "fabulous" and "brilliant" and asked for more covers along the same lines.

Early in 1966, Rosemary Frank, who had recently begun supervising TIME's cover-making process, wrote a memo that sought to introduce yet another new wrinkle to the newsmaker portrait *(fig. 27)*. She suggested that a good artist for the upcoming cover of Broadway producer David Merrick would be Marisol (Escobar), that "far out Venezuelan-American sculptress with the long black hair."

On that occasion TIME opted for another artist. Once mentioned, however, Marisol's

Fig. 27

Cover coordinator Rosemary Frank, 1968.
Photograph by Martha Holmes

name was not forgotten, and the next year she was commissioned to do the cover portrait of Hugh Hefner, founder of the hugely successful men's magazine *Playboy (page 78)*. In Marisol's hands, the portrait took on a startlingly three-dimensional twist. There was Hefner, "the country's leading impresario of spectator sex," with his red-sweatered figure painted on a wooden box, his head formed from a laminated wooden block that the artist had intentionally shaped along the lines of a jet engine, and puffing on one of his trademark pipes while holding a second.

Marisol was elusive when it came to explaining this composition. She could not say why Hefner's head was shaped like a jet engine, and when asked the meaning of the red, white, and blue of Hefner's boxy body, her answer was tentative: "Perhaps he's the all-American boy." But on the question of what the two pipes meant, she was clear: Hefner, she declared, "has too much of everything."

Unlike so many other images that departed from TIME's cover norm, Marisol's *Hefner* does not seem to have drawn any strong reader objection on aesthetic grounds. In fact, the only communication on the cover that TIME saw fit to publish in its letters section came from a woman who declared it a very apt rendering of a man who was, after all, "an absurd, gutless, blockheaded monster." But while Marisol's *Hefner* was a portrait that at least one of his

detractors could love, it was something that Hefner admired as well, so much so that he tried to interest Marisol in doing another portrait of him for himself.

Among the most memorable indications in the late 1960s of the escalating eclecticism in covers was TIME's portrait of the Beatles in September 1967 *(pages 76–77)*. In early discussions on who would do the Beatles' cover portrait, the group's British origins gave rise to the thought of asking a British cartoonist to supply it. Cover coordinator Rosemary Frank gathered information on a number of likely candidates, among them Gerald Scarfe, who, she warned in a memo, sometimes "goes a little too far." Still, she added, "he['s] my favorite if we could control him." Frank probably was right to worry a bit about Scarfe's tendencies to go over the top. Described as the "most savagely satirical political cartoonist in Britain," he could be devastatingly cruel. But if there were grounds for concern about Scarfe, it is also understandable why he was ultimately chosen. Above all, he was ingeniously clever.

Going on life sketches he made of the Beatles at home and in a rehearsal, Scarfe fashioned their images in papier-mâché at roughly life size. Then he clothed the waist-length figures in apparel evoking the Beatles' interest in Eastern music and philosophy—George Harrison in patterned Indian cotton, Ringo Starr in a silk tweed, John Lennon in a gold-and-silver embroidered coat, and Paul McCartney in a jacket made from ninety-eight-dollar-a-yard gold-threaded fabric originally destined for a dethroned Dalai Lama. By the time the last daub of paint was applied and the figures were properly arranged, the overall effect was spectacular. While the satiric edge in the facial expressions proved more endearing than acerbic, the composition possessed an overall sense of animation capable of producing a momentary illusion that if you listened hard enough, you might actually hear the figures sing.

One of the factors behind TIME's growing cover variety in the late sixties was the notion that greater consideration should be given to finding artists whose interests and preferences meshed particularly well with given subjects.

One of the clearest instances occurred in the spring of 1967, when TIME was looking forward to a summer cover story on the freewheeling hippie youth culture taking hold across the country. On this occasion it was thought that the best artist for doing a cover would be one who knew it firsthand, and the magazine opted for a group of hippie artists who, in keeping with the egalitarian communalism of their movement, produced the cover as a collective effort *(fig. 28)*. They were part of a commune in Manhattan's East Village called Group Image, which produced art, music, and the magazine *Innerspace*, and eschewed the use of last names because it called too much attention to individual identities.

Hearing that their cover image had been accepted, the spokesman for the contributing artists adamantly refused to be awed by the accomplishment, remarking, "Well, we try to take everything in stride. Six months ago I might have thought it was the greatest thing; now it's not the greatest thing, it's not the smallest thing either, but just another thing." He then went on to observe that there were some who were a little surprised that Group Image would work for such a "straight" publication. On that point he was philosophically tolerant, saying, "We recognize the straight world." Besides, he added, the money would come in handy.[40]

Another cover that attempted to match the right artist to the right subject was the likeness of Robert Kennedy by Roy Lichtenstein that ran shortly before Kennedy's assassination during his campaign for the Democratic presidential nomination of 1968 *(page 82)*. Heir to his brother John's charismatic mantle, Robert Kennedy definitely had the makings of a political folk hero, with his hard-driving style, impassioned profession of concern for have-nots, and youthful vitality. There was, therefore, no more appropriate artist for a Kennedy cover than Lichtenstein, whose works, patterned on comic book illustrations were hallmarks of the current pop art movement. What better way to underscore Kennedy's emerging larger-than-life persona than to depict him as a comic strip superhero?

Two responses of TIME readers to this first instance of a newsmaker being rendered in a comic book style are most interesting when read in succession, as the magazine printed them. The author of the first applauded Lichtenstein for showing Kennedy up to be the "comic, callow and caustic" fellow that he was. The author of the second response hailed the image because it showed Kennedy as a "great leader," exploding with "youth, nationalism, pride and determination."

One of TIME's finest meshes between subject and artist almost didn't come off. The subject was Hollywood actor John Wayne, whose triumph in 1969 as the dusty, eye-patched hero of the western *True Grit* climaxed his long career as America's best-known screen cowboy. The artist was Harry Jackson, a one-time abstract expressionist who ultimately found his proper artistic milieu when he turned

Fig. 28
Group Image. The Hippies. TIME, July 7, 1967

to sculpting the western cowboy in the tradition of Frederic Remington.

To woo a reluctant Jackson into doing an equestrian Wayne in his *True Grit* character, TIME bent over backward. After agreeing to let Jackson produce replicas of the final likeness to market as he wished—a proposition that would normally have been rejected out of hand—the magazine hired a studio for Jackson in New York City and an assistant for him. But it seemed that all this special treatment would end in disaster when an anxious Jackson suddenly contracted a severe case of loss of confidence. Complaining that he was too tired, he was sure he could not finish Wayne in time for the magazine's deadline.

The deadline was met, just barely, thanks in large part to Rosemary Frank, who served as the artist's hand-holder and morale-booster as he raced to finish the piece during a modeling session that lasted until three in the morning. As it was, Jackson did not complete the piece in those wee hours, but he had gotten far enough in molding his original model in painted wax that from certain angles it looked finished and could be photographed for the cover *(pages 88–89)*.

Another memorable application of the "right-artist/right-subject" principle was the 1969 cover of movie sex symbol Raquel Welch. Since the unabashedly sensual Rita Hayworth cover by George Petty in 1941, TIME seemed to have consciously shied away from newsmaker likenesses that trafficked heavily in sex appeal. Even Marilyn Monroe's cover image of 1956 had made her out to be little more than an unusually attractive example of the girl next door. The new sexual openness of the late 1960s, however, loosened the constraints on cover sexuality, and in the summer of 1969, when TIME looked ahead to an upcoming feature story on Welch, it was assumed from the start that her sexual attraction would be the focus of her cover image. The magazine called upon a master in capturing female physical allure, sculptor Frank Gallo. His *Welch* produced the desired effect and then some *(page 86)*. Certainly there was no confusing this bikini-clad siren with the girl next door.

One of the reader reactions to this cover came from a man in Iowa who seemed to be less disturbed with the Welch likeness itself and more with the fact that it had been featured on the cover of a serious newsmagazine. "I received your Nov. 28 issue of PlayTIME," he wrote. "My copy does not contain the middle foldout. Will you please send? For your information, three astronauts flew to the moon that week. I cannot remember their names, but maybe you can get the information from Hugh Hefner." But that response was only the tip of the iceberg. Of the more than nine hundred readers sending in reactions to the cover, nearly 100 percent—invoking terms such as "utterly tasteless" and "new low"—were vehemently negative. Thus it seemed that the new tolerance for sexual frankness had its limits, and as far as a lot of TIME readers were concerned, the cover of their favorite newsweekly did not fall within them.

For many years it would never have dawned on TIME to resort to the editorial cartoon and caricature tradition for covers featuring political figures. Behind this was the thought that the cover is essentially neutral territory, not an opinion page. But by the early seventies, political cartooning was very much a component of the growing diversity of TIME covers, though care was taken that the satirical flavor of an image was reasonably mild and bipartisan. In 1968, for example, when Gerald Scarfe presented TIME with his commissioned papier-mâché rendering of Richard Nixon, based on impressions gathered while traveling with Nixon on the presidential campaign trail, the magazine regarded the piece's satiric bite as too strong by half and rejected it.

Although TIME's cover ventures into political satire and caricature were of the gentler sort, that did not mean that they were blandly dull. To the contrary, their humorous imagery made for some of the magazine's most effective and informative covers, and some of the covers distilled the stories that ran with them pretty comprehensively. One example was Jack Davis's cover for one of TIME's earliest stories on the Watergate scandals *(page 93)*. Published in April 1973 with the caption headline "Watergate Breaks Wide Open," the piece offered perhaps as good a summation as any single picture could of the recent string of events that were beginning to disclose Watergate's complicated web of wrongdoing. Without reading a word of the cover story itself, it was possible to understand its basic thrust by looking at Davis's image of Nixon's advisers implicated in Watergate, all pointing accusatory fingers at each other.

Interestingly enough, the liveliness and wit of cartoon covers does not necessarily appeal to casual magazine buyers. At least that would seem to be the case, judging from an eight-year survey of TIME newsstand sales spanning the late 1970s and early 1980s, which also disclosed, among other things, that female cover subjects sold better than male subjects. Cartoon covers ranked right up along with economy-oriented ones as the most likely to dampen newsstand sales. "Cartoons sell awful," as managing editor Ray Cave put it. Photographic covers broke down newsstand sales resistance much more readily.[41]

Newsstand sales have always represented a fairly small portion of TIME's total circulation, the bulk of which is by subscription. Thus the correlation between cover type and newsstand sales has never strongly determined the covers. Nevertheless, by the early 1980s photography was increasingly the favored cover medium, and by the early 1990s more than half of a given year's cover output would be photographic.

The list of photographers who have done covers for TIME in the past two or three decades is long and includes some of the most distinguished studio and news photographers of the modern day, among them Richard Avedon, Irving Penn, Frank Scavullo, Eddie Adams, and David Hume Kennerly. Among the most frequently represented was Neil Leifer, who began his career as a sports photographer. His sensible, hardworking father took a dim view of his teenaged son's desire to make his living snapping pictures of people playing games. But then he learned that the fees his boy earned for just three images shot at a single baseball game equaled the hefty $450 price of the new Nikon camera with which he had taken them. With that, parental disapproval ceased to be a roadblock in Leifer's career. As a *Sports Illustrated*

staffer, he won a reputation as "one of the masters of sports photography."[42]

After Leifer joined TIME in the late 1970s, the magazine naturally tapped his visual expertise in matters athletic by assigning him to sporting events. But he also covered many other fronts as well, and among the most ingenious cover images he produced for the magazine was one of New York City's feisty mayor Ed Koch, who was posed on a tugboat in the East River, creating the illusion that Koch was a good-natured giant looming convivially above Manhattan's skyline *(fig. 29)*. His most original cover, technically, was of the legendary football coach of the University of Alabama, Paul "Bear" Bryant *(page 103)*. The portrait showed Bryant, white chalk in hand, seeming to be contemplating game plays on an opaque blackboard, which, oddly, serves as a mirror for Bryant's features, an impression created by painstakingly orchestrated double-exposure sleight of hand that Leifer had been perfecting for many years.

Another photographer doing covers for TIME in recent years is William Coupon. Shortly after graduating from Syracuse University in the mid-1970s, Coupon settled in Manhattan, where he first made his name as a chronicler of the punk movement just as it was reaching its height. From the start, his central interest was portraiture, and he adopted a style that bespoke a reverence for Rembrandt that was achieved largely through strong single-source lighting and spare, neutral backdrops. The result was dramatically shadowed likenesses having a distinctly painterly feel.

Coupon's formulaic approach might seem bound to produce portraits that begin to look alike. But Coupon defends his format, claiming that while it is "respectful" of sitters, it also stands a better chance than other photographic styles of yielding "a more revealing portrait" of their individuality.[43] Coupon has a point: the compositional predictability simply puts in high relief the personality he seeks to capture. His painterly simplicity, moreover, makes for a particularly happy blend with TIME's red-bordered format with its bold logo, and of the magazine's photographic covers of the 1980s and early 1990s, many of his newsmaker likenesses are among the most satisfying.

A common element in many portraitists' memoirs is a preference for taking time in the portrait-making process to get to know subjects through conversation. Behind that strategy, of course, is the notion that the better one knows the subject, the more insightful and penetrating the likeness will be. Coupon, however, does not share that preference. Subscribing to the motto "less said, the better," he speaks to his subjects "very rarely."[44] Moreover, he works with remarkable speed. When, for example, he went down to Little Rock, Arkansas, to shoot President-elect Bill Clinton's 1992 Man of the Year cover, he was all business. At the end of seven minutes of photographing Clinton against a portable beige backdrop, he had shot six rolls of film and told Clinton, "I think I got it." Used to cutting short sessions with photographers who wanted more time with him than he was willing to give, an astonished Clinton dubbed Coupon "the first photographer I didn't stop first."[45]

Greg Heisler, another TIME cover photographer, has no distinctive style. As Heisler himself once put it, "I don't get hired to do a 'Greg Heisler picture'—for the simple reason that there isn't such a thing." Instead, as he sees it, his clients hire him "to solve the puzzle of a particular job."[46] The subject of his first TIME cover was movie and TV director/writer David Lynch, whose taste for the bizarre and surreally gruesome yielded in 1990 the hit television series *Twin Peaks*. At a glance, it would seem that Heisler sought to underscore Lynch's offbeat creative nature simply by casting an eerie green shadow over half of his subject's face. But closer scrutiny reveals a far weirder effect. Through double exposure, he melded two shots of Lynch, and while one eye looks squarely at the viewer, the other looks worriedly to the side. The impression created by this seamless duality is that Heisler somehow caught in his lens a schizophrenic shifting from one aspect of his personality to another *(page 123)*.

Heisler's 1991 Man of the Year cover of cable television mogul Ted Turner also relied on illusion. This time, however, he achieved it through digital imaging. Among the first in his profession to begin exploring the computer's potential in the

Fig. 29
Neil Leifer. Ed Koch. TIME, June 15, 1981

late 1980s, he labored over the picture for two weeks. But the final image did not betray his keyboard toil, having all the slickness of a magic trick as Turner's disembodied face emerges, Oz-like, from between two halves of a floating globe paved with television screens *(fig. 30)*.

Perhaps the most noticeable change in the TIME cover tradition since the mid-1960s has been a fundamental shift in subject matter. Founded by two men who believed in Thomas Carlyle's notion that history is the story of great individuals, the magazine for decades let that notion dictate the subject matter for most covers—images of noted personalities who were exercising an impact on their age. But in the late 1960s newsworthy issues and situations seemed to be emerging that were more collective in nature and did not readily lend themselves to the personality-oriented reportorial approach. At TIME the trend away from an emphasis on personality received impetus from Henry Grunwald, who became managing editor in 1968 and who in many respects encouraged the orientation toward issues. As a result, occasions grew in number when TIME's long-standing newsmaker cover formula was inappropriate, and by the early 1970s cover portraits of identifiable individuals were losing ground to issue-oriented covers on topics and themes such as "Blue-Collar Power," "Inefficient America," or "U.S. Inflation." By the early 1990s, newsmaker portraits and more topically oriented imagery were sharing the magazine's weekly covers on a roughly equal basis.

Among the wittiest topical covers from the past three decades were several that were the work of the Belgian-born, Paris-based artist Jean-Michel Folon, known for surrealistic satire of contemporary life. In August 1979 he supplied TIME with "Topsy-Turvy Economy" to run with a story focused on the combination of chronic inflation and stagnation that was plaguing the United States. In this delicately drawn watercolor, he depicted Uncle Sam rolling passively across a spare, gently sloped landscape, creating a quietly amusing, but nevertheless sharp, distillation of the ineffectiveness that characterized U.S. policymakers' response to the country's economic woes.

There have been moments at TIME when the task of coming up with an acceptable cover on a given subject seemed almost impossible. In 1969 the magazine planned a feature on the sexual frankness that was manifesting itself in everything from mainstream films to an increasingly open marketing of hard-core pornography in print. While TIME wanted an image that addressed this explicitness in a lively manner, its editorial and art staffs did not want the cover of their weekly newsmagazine to adopt the titillating look of a sex magazine. The solution, Rosemary Frank recalled, required "a lot of hard thinking," and in the process a number of proposed concepts bit the dust.[47] Finally an illustrator named Dennis Wheeler, who had begun doing covers for the magazine the previous year, came up with an answer that sent TIME staffers scurrying to the Brooklyn Botanic Gardens and a Manhattan notions sales counter. While the former supplied a fig leaf, the latter yielded a zipper, and when these two items were coyly combined to shield most of the nakedness of two cast members from the largely nude New York theater revue *Oh! Calcutta!* the result was

an image that struck a playfully suggestive note without offending anyone's sense of newsmagazine decorum.

The topical issue that was most difficult to translate into a cover was TIME's 1966 examination of the ongoing debate over the existence of God and whether, as the German philosopher Friedrich Nietzsche had asserted many years earlier, contentious and self-absorbed mankind had finally made him irrelevant. The search for a cover that addressed such a sensitive question and, at the same time, minimized the risk of adverse reader reaction began roughly a year before the story ran. When it was done, Rosemary Frank, who had been in on the quest from the outset, described it as "the walk through the valley of the shadow."

The various artists consulted were baffled at the prospect of creating such a cover; some thought that it was an exercise in "how not to say something."[48] Many pieces of already existing art came under consideration, such as Abraham Rattner's *Window Cleaner*, which showed a shadowy figure barely discernible through a stained-glass window. But in every case the artwork was, for one reason or another, dismissed as inappropriate. A host of museum directors and religious leaders were also asked for advice, and pleas went out to the magazine's foreign bureaus for assistance in ferreting out the possible existence of some overlooked religious image that might suit the occasion.

Among the artists willing to take a stab at this cover was Larry Rivers, who at one point seemed to offer the best hope for a satisfactory image. After a couple of conferences with Henry Grunwald, Rivers set about creating a cover collage that placed significant classical religious imagery in a modern context. Like the other artists who had accepted this assignment, however, he failed to come up with a satisfactory piece.

When the issue carrying the story came off the press in April 1966, it had a cover like no other before it. Originally suggested as a last-ditch solution by managing editor Otto Fuerbringer, the image consisted simply of three words in bold red type set against a black background: "Is God Dead?" *(fig. 31).* For the first time in the magazine's history, its cover was, in

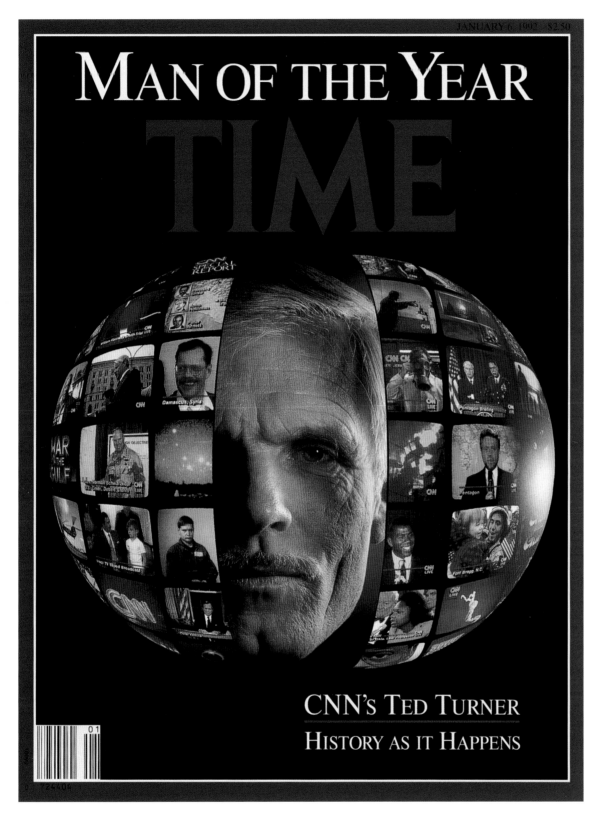

MAN OF THE YEAR

TIME

CNN's TED TURNER
HISTORY AS IT HAPPENS

Fig. 30
Greg Heisler. Ted Turner.
TIME, January 6, 1992

short, pictureless. Even a pictureless cover, however, had its critics. "Your ugly cover," one reader said, "is a blasphemous outrage and, appearing as it does during Passover and Easter week, an affront to every believing Jew and Christian." On the other hand, there were those who considered it a stroke of genius. "May I compliment you on your excellent cover,"

Fig. 31
Charles Jackson.
Is God Dead? TIME,
April 8, 1966

wrote one. "The simple wording and boldness of it provoke in themselves great thought."

Although issue-oriented nonportrait covers had by the early 1990s substantially displaced the once overwhelmingly prevalent newsmaker likenesses, TIME's close identification with portrait images of the world's powerful and famous continued unchanged in the public mind. Also unchanged was the popular mythos that had over seven decades come to engulf those portrait images. An especially telling case in point was Dick Morris, who was chief strategist for President Clinton's 1996 reelection campaign until a prostitute told of Morris's trysts with her in a posh Washington hotel suite on the eve of Clinton's convention nomination. TIME ran Morris on its cover, in tandem with Clinton, just as the 1996 Democratic National Convention was calling its first sessions to order. When the news of Morris's dalliance became public and forced his resignation, the magazine decided to run him on the cover again, this time pictured with his wife, who, for the time being at least, was standing foursquare beside him. Until this point, hardly anyone outside of high political circles knew who Dick Morris was. But now his name was plastered on front pages of newspapers across the country. And what, one may ask, was the gauge invoked to measure Morris's phenomenal overnight fame? For pundit after pundit, in news columns and on television, it was that Morris had the distinction, shared by very few others, of having appeared on the cover of TIME for two weeks in a row.

However much TIME's cover style and subject matter have changed over the years, there seems to be one unalterable truth: being on the cover of TIME remains a popular shorthand symbol of "making it, big time." For some cover subjects, however, it is a question not just of "making it," but of making it for the right reasons. When Pope John Paul II was being interviewed for his 1994 Man of the Year article, he puckishly noted that he would be assuming a title once claimed by Stalin and Hitler. "Holy Father," the TIME correspondent hastened to explain, "you must understand that we have a good list and a bad list. You are on the good list." To which the pontiff playfully replied, "I hope I always remain on the good list."

NOTES

1. Robert Elson, *Time Inc.: The History of a Publishing Enterprise* (New York: Atheneum, 1968), pp. 85–86; W. A. Swanberg, *Luce and His Empire* (New York: Charles Scribner's Sons, 1972), p. 62.

2. TIME, April 30, 1965, p. 25.

3. TIME, April 7, 1930, p. 4.

4. Notes on conversation with Robert Woods, February 15, 1996, TIME Collection files, National Portrait Gallery, Smithsonian Institution, Washington, D.C.

5. TIME, April 30, 1956, p. 15.

6. Samuel J. Woolf, *Here I Am* (New York: Random House, 1941), p. 70.

7. Ibid., p. 145.

8. Ibid., p. 96.

9. TIME, November 24, 1941, pp. 13–14; December 1, 1941, p. 9.

10. Guy Rowe, "Those TIME Covers by Baker," *The American Artist* (February 1943), p. 31.

11. TIME, March 27, 1939, p. 8.

12. TIME, June 30, 1941, p. 8.

13. The accounts of the events leading to Artzybasheff's immigration to the United States vary considerably in their details. The story given here is drawn from a typed memoir by Artzybasheff, found in his papers at the Syracuse University Library, which strikes this writer as probably the most accurate.

14. TIME, July 3, 1944, p. 13.

15. Ibid.

16. *Notebook #1*, 1958–1962, entry on cover portrait of General Kong Le, published June 26, 1964, Boris Artzybasheff papers, Syracuse University Library.

17. TIME, September 21, 1942, p. 21.

18. Videotape interview with John Hersey, September 27, 1991, National Portrait Gallery, Smithsonian Institution.

19. TIME, November 27, 1933, p. 2.

20. TIME, January 18, 1937, p. 4.

21. TIME, January 16, 1939, p. 9.

22. Ray Hoopes, *Ralph Ingersoll* (New York: Atheneum, 1985), p. 182.

23. TIME, January 25, 1943, p. 10.

24. Draft of letter, Ernest Hamlin Baker to John Valentine, undated [April/May 1942], photocopy, TIME Collection files, National Portrait Gallery, Smithsonian Institution.

25. Robert Weldy Baer to Ernest Hamlin Baker, undated [January 1951], photocopy, TIME Collection files, National Portrait Gallery, Smithsonian Institution.

26. TIME, January 12, 1962, p. 2; January 19, 1962, p. 6.

27. TIME, January 19, 1962, p. 11.

28. David Halberstam, *The Powers That Be* (New York: Alfred A. Knopf, 1979), p. 359.

29. Conversation with Joseph Bowler, June 5, 1996, TIME Collection files, National Portrait Gallery, Smithsonian Institution.

30. TIME, January 14, 1980, p. 4; January 21, 1980, p. 10.

31. Hedley Donovan, *Right Places, Right Times* (New York: Henry Holt and Company, 1989), p. 326.

32. TIME, January 7, 1991, p. 15.

33. *New York Times*, June 27, 1991.

34. Susan Heller Anderson, "Chronicle," *New York Times*, June 27, 1991.

35. TIME, August 8, 1955, p. 2.

36. *Art News*, February 1948, p. 49; TIME, January 5, 1948, p. 53.

37. Brochure for TIME cover exhibition, September 1963.

38. Unpublished reminiscence of Henry Koerner, TIME Collection files, National Portrait Gallery, Smithsonian Institution.

39. *Recent Paintings by Robert Vickrey* (New York: Kennedy Galleries, Inc., 1990), p. 1.

40. Rosemary Frank to Henry Grunwald, July 1 [1967], TIME Collection files, National Portrait Gallery, Smithsonian Institution.

41. Ray Cave, "Cave's Commandment: Thou Shalt Not McJournal the News," *Quill* (July/August 1987), p. 17.

42. "Neil Leifer," *American Photo* 2, no. 4 (July/August 1991), p. 67.

43. TIME, January 4, 1993, p. 4.

44. Larry Frascella, "William Coupon," *Communication Arts* 31 (September/October 1989), p. 50.

45. TIME, January 4, 1993, p. 4.

46. Laurence Shames, "Professionally Tailored: Gregory Heisler and the Photographic Revolution of End Use," *American Photographer* (August 1986), p. 42.

47. Memo, Rosemary Frank to Henry Grunwald, August 4, 1970, TIME Collection files, National Portrait Gallery, Smithsonian Institution.

48. Copy of memo, Rosemary Frank to Frank Shea, March 30, 1966. TIME Collection files, National Portrait Gallery, Smithsonian Institution.

PLATES

Unless otherwise noted,

all artworks are in the collection of, or on loan to,

the National Portrait Gallery, Smithsonian Institution, Washington, D.C.

Names of donors or lenders of specific works are given

in the checklist of the exhibition, page 129.

Text accompanying an artwork appeared originally in the issue of TIME

for which the artwork was the cover illustration.

Charles A. Lindbergh
May. 27, 1927

CHARLES LINDBERGH
Man of the Year

by Samuel J. Woolf
(1880–1948)

charcoal on paper,
33.6 x 28.8 cm
(13¼ x 11¼ in.)

TIME, January 2, 1928

HEROES
Lindbergh

Height: 6 ft. 2 inches.
Age: 25.
Eyes: Blue.
Cheeks: Pink.
Hair: Sandy.

Feet: Large. When he arrived at the Embassy in France no shoes big enough were handy. Habits: Smokes not; drinks not. Does not gamble. Eats a thorough-going breakfast. Prefers light luncheon and dinner when permitted. Avoids rich dishes. Likes sweets.

Calligraphy: From examination of his handwriting Dr. Camille Streletski, Secretary of the French Graphological Society, concluded: superiority, intellectualism, cerebration, idealism, even mysticism.

Characteristics: Modesty, taciturnity, diffidence (women make him blush), singleness of purpose, courage, occasional curtness, phlegm. Elinor Glyn avers he lacks "It."

HENRY PU YI

by Jerry Farnsworth
(1895–1982)

oil on board, 36.2 x 30.5 cm
(14¼ x 12¹⁄₁₆ in.)

TIME, March 5, 1934

In the bitter cold of Manchuria great things were about to happen. . . . Blinking, bespectacled Henry Pu Yi was about to become Manchu emperor of the new state of Ta Manchu Tikuo, until last week Manchukuo. . . . Only 28 years old, Henry Pu Yi is no stranger to thrones. Twice before he has been proclaimed emperor of China. The first time was when he was two years old. . . . In 1917 he became Emperor Hsuan Tung again for a few days when swashbuckling General Hsun . . . captured Peiping, and popped him on the throne in the middle of a July night. . . .

All his life a helpless tool of one agency or another, Pu Yi has longed to dodge the trappings of state and lead the life of a normal western youth. . . . Bicycling is one of his hobbies. As a Japanese puppet he dares not leave his palace unguarded, so he rides around and around his garden compound doing tricks. The emperor of Manchukuo can now pedal on the rear wheel alone, with the front wheel in the air.

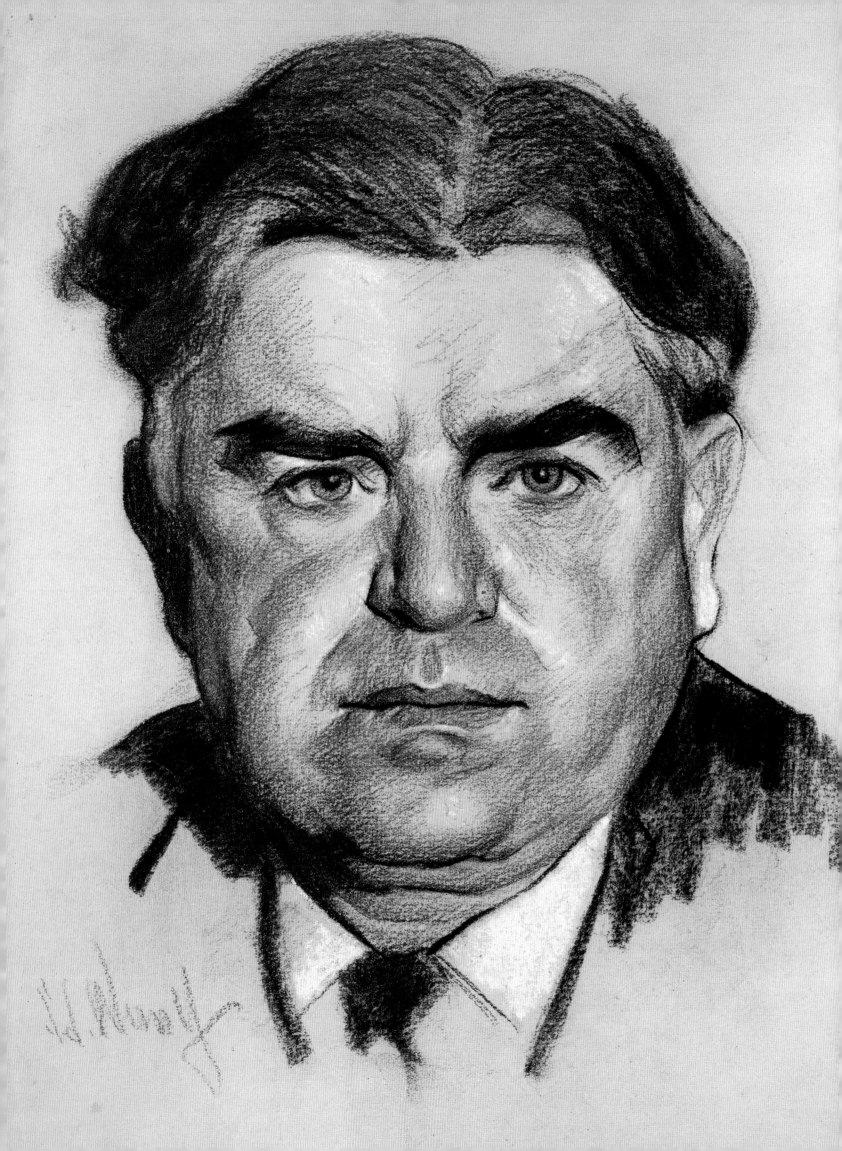

JOHN L. LEWIS

by Samuel J. Woolf
(1880–1948)

charcoal on paper, 32.8 x 27 cm
(12¹⁵⁄₁₆ x 10⅝ in.)

TIME, October 2, 1933

"We will now hear from the
president of the United Mine
Workers of America."
    . . . Everyone in the hall knew the
squat, bull-necked, heavy-pawed
figure that swaggered out to the
rostrum. There was a glint of
arrogance in his grey eyes. He
jutted his heavy jaw. Dramatically
he introduced himself in the idiom
of the true labor leader:
"The name is Lewis—John L."

GERTRUDE STEIN

by George Platt Lynes
(1907–1955)

gelatin silver print, 35.3 x 28.1 cm
(13⅞ x 10¹⁄₁₆ in.)

TIME, September 11, 1933

. . . the plain reader dips into
another Stein volume (*Tender Buttons*),
to his astonishment brings up these:
"*Red Roses*. A cool red rose and
a pink cut pink, a collapse and a
sold hole, a little less hot.
"*A Sound*. Elephant beaten with
candy and little pops and chews
all bolts and reckless rats, this is
this. . . .
"*Chicken*. Alas a dirty word, alas
a dirty third, alas a dirty bird."
    Some readers laugh, some are
annoyed; some snort with disgust
or indignation. Gertrude Stein,
writer for posterity ("I write for
myself and strangers") does not
mind. Says she slyly: "My sentences
do get under their skin. . . ."

ADMIRAL OSAMI NAGANO

by Boris Artzybasheff
(1899–1965)

gouache on board, 26.6 x 23.3 cm
(10½ x 9³⁄₁₆ in.)

TIME, February 15, 1943

CHIEF OF NAVAL GENERAL STAFF, JAPAN

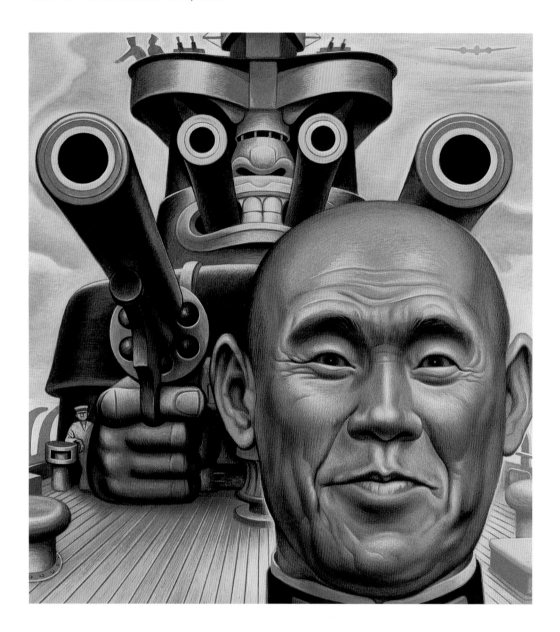

GRAND ADMIRAL KARL DOENITZ

by Boris Artzybasheff
(1899–1965)

gouache on board, 26.8 x 23.9 cm
(10⁹⁄₁₆ x 9⁷⁄₁₆ in.)

TIME, May 10, 1943

COMMANDER IN CHIEF OF THE GERMAN NAVY

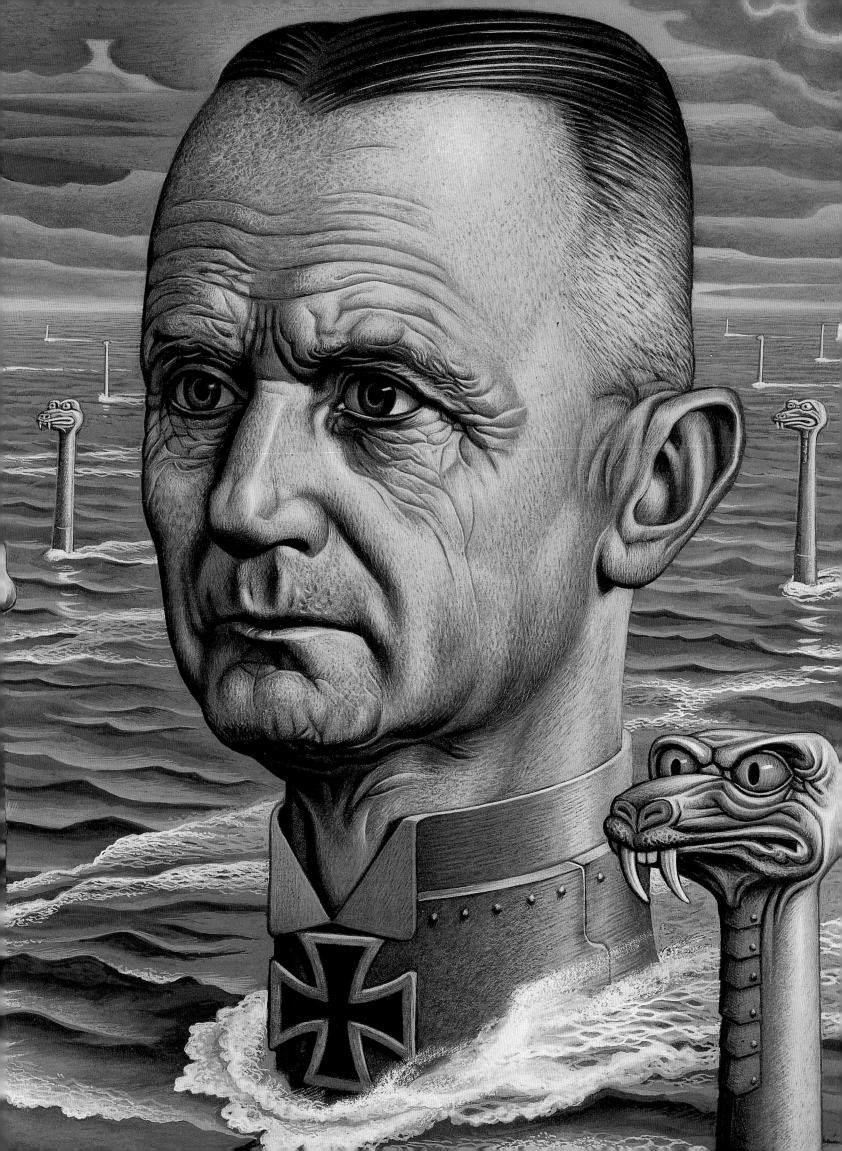

MARSHAL TITO

by Boris Chaliapin
(1904–1979)

gouache on board,
30.4 x 27.2 cm (12 x 10¾ in.)

TIME, October 9, 1944

Word spread through the hills, towns and cities: a remarkable Croat named Tito was fighting the Germans. Yugoslavs from all classes and political parties joined him. . . .

The blacksmith's boy from Klanjec had become leader of a resistance movement that at one time or another pinned down as many as 18 German divisions in fruitless, fraying warfare in the wild Croation and Bosnian mountains.

GENERAL SIR BERNARD LAW MONTGOMERY

by Boris Chaliapin
(1904–1979)

gouache on board, 30.5 x 27.5 cm
(12¹⁄₁₆ x 10⅞ in.)

TIME, February 1, 1943

[Montgomery's] Eighth Army, after some of the bitterest fighting that Egypt had seen, had cracked the Afrika Corps. Newsmen met Montgomery in his desert headquarters. He sat through the interview with a fly whisk balanced steadily on one finger. "I have defeated the enemy. I am now about to smash him," he asserted flatly, relaxed and asked: "How do you like my hat?" Then wearing a tank corps beret which he had picked up, he climbed into a tank and rumbled off after his troops like a skinny avenging angel.

LIEUTENANT GENERAL JONATHAN WAINWRIGHT

by Ernest Hamlin Baker
(1889–1975)

gouache on board,
25.4 x 22.8 cm (10 x 9 in.)

TIME, May 8, 1944

Shortly before noon, [the] commander of U.S. forces in the Philippines left his headquarters on the stricken island. Wainwright walked toward his conquerors (reported *Nichi Nichi*'s correspondent), carrying a white flag. He "slumped into a chair . . . head held in both hands, his eyes staring at the ground." When the victorious Japanese commander entered the room, "Wainwright and his aides stood up at rigid attention and saluted.". . . It was Corregidor's end. The day was May 6, 1942.

ALBERT EINSTEIN

by Ernest Hamlin Baker
(1889–1975)

gouache on board,
32.8 x 29.2 cm (13 x 11½ in.)

TIME, July 1, 1946

Einstein's discoveries, the greatest
triumph of reasoning mind on
record, are accepted by most
people on faith. Hence the fact
that most people never expect to
understand more about Relativity
than is told by the limerick:

There was a young lady called
* Bright,*
Who could travel much faster
* than light;*
She went out one day,
In a relative way,
And came back the previous night.

WINSTON CHURCHILL
Man of the Half-Century

by Ernest Hamlin Baker
(1889–1975)

gouache on board,
29.8 x 26.7 cm (11¾ x 10½ in.)

TIME, January 2, 1950

The personal Churchill was happy,
reveling in the good things of life,
both the simple and the complex.
He laid bricks and built dams at
his country home, enjoyed the best
food and sampled, thoroughly,
the best brandy. From painting, for
years his main hobby, he derived
"a tremendous new pleasure."
Only Winston Churchill could have
said: "Painting a picture is like
fighting a battle. . . . It is the same
kind of problem as unfolding a long,
sustained, interlocked argument."

MARIA CALLAS

by Henry Koerner
(1915–1991)

oil on canvas, 55.9 x 71.1 cm
(22 x 28 in.)

TIME, October 29, 1956

Few rate the Callas voice as
opera's sweetest or most
beautiful. It has its ravishing
moments. In quiet passages, it
warms and caresses the air.
In ensembles, it cuts through
the other voices like a
Damascus blade, clean and
strong. . . . But the special
quality of the Callas voice is
not tone. It is the extraordinary
ability to carry, as can no
other, the inflections and
nuances of emotion, from
mordant intensity to hushed
delicacy.

WILLIAM HARTACK

by James Chapin
(1887–1975)

oil on canvas, 51.1 x 35.9 cm
(20⅛ x 14⅛ in.)

TIME, February 10, 1958

If jockeys had their own
colors, his would have to be
red (for guts) and green
(for money).

CHARLES DE GAULLE
Man of the Year

*by Bernard Buffet
(born 1928)*

*oil on canvas,
101 x 74.2 cm
(39¾ x 29¼ in.)*

TIME, January 5, 1959

DE GAULLE ON FRANCE:
"The emotional side of me tends to imagine France, like the princess in the fairy stories or the Madonna in the frescoes, as dedicated to an exalted and exceptional destiny. Instinctively I have the feeling that Providence has created her either for complete successes or for exemplary misfortunes. . . . In short, to my mind, France cannot be France without greatness."

DWIGHT D. EISENHOWER

*by Andrew Wyeth
(born 1917)*

*tempera and dry brush on paper,
26.7 x 24.8 cm
(10½ x 9¾ in.)*

TIME, September 7, 1959
Los Angeles County Museum of Art; gift of Dwight D. Eisenhower (M.A.)

Ike had always liked Wyeth's work. . . . He found he liked Wyeth's gentle, almost courtly manners too, and permitted him to spend five full days working at Gettysburg. . . . At Wyeth's request Ike donned his favorite jacket, a straw-colored, nubby silk. He sat unsmiling and as if alone with his thoughts. Previous portraitists, working mostly from photographs, have tended to crystallize the popular image of a beamingly paternal president. Wyeth saw and showed an elderly, strong-minded, dedicated public servant, calm in the vortex of great events.

JOHN F. KENNEDY
Man of the Year

*by Pietro Annigoni
(1910–1988)*

*watercolor on paper, 78.5 x 58.7 cm
(30⅞ x 23⅛ in.)*

TIME, January 5, 1962

Jack Kennedy . . . had passionately sought the presidency. The closeness of his victory did not disturb him; he took over the office with a youth-can-do-anything sort of self-confidence. He learned better; but learn he did. . . . He also made the process of his growing up to be president a saving factor for the U.S. in the cold war.

POPE JOHN XXIII

*by Pietro Annigoni
(1910–1988)*

*charcoal on paper, 61.6 x 50.1 cm
(24¼ x 19¾ in.)*

TIME, October 5, 1962

The purpose of the Second Vatican Council is what His Holiness Pope John XXIII, who has the Catholic prelate's traditional wariness of words that suggest drastic change, calls an *aggiornamento*—a moderniza- tion. This self-reform will affect the life, the worship, and the discipline of every Catholic; just as importantly, it will affect the way the church looks to other Christians, and to the world at large. It is the hope of Pope John, and of many of his bishops, that the Protestant and Orthodox churches will be favorably impressed, and that Catholicism may be pointed toward the far-distant goal of nearly all Christians: their ultimate unity in one church.

VII - VI - LXII
in Vaticano

MARTIN LUTHER KING, JR.

by Ben Shahn
(1898–1969)

pen, ink, and wash on
Japanese paper,
66.6 x 51.7 cm
(26¼ x 20⅜ in.)

TIME, March 19, 1965

Amon Carter Museum,
Fort Worth, Texas

Ben Shahn is as famed in his own medium of protest as King is in his. Lately he has been contributing posters and lithographs to various civil rights groups. . . . He saw his subject mainly as an orator. "This is King today," he said. "He isn't as placid as he was a year ago. I admire the man immensely. He has moved more people by his oratory than anyone else I can think of."

MARTIN LUTHER KING, JR.
Man of the Year

by Robert Vickrey
(born 1926)

tempera on paper, 37.5 x 28.5 cm
(14¾ x 11¼ in.)

TIME, January 3, 1964

BUCKMINSTER FULLER

by Boris Artzybasheff
(1899–1965)

tempera on board,
54.6 x 43.2 cm (21½ x 17 in.)

TIME, January 10, 1964

He has been called "the first poet
of technology," "the greatest living
genius of industrial-technical
realization in building," "an
anticipator of the world to come—
which is different from being a
prophet," "a seminal thinker," and
"an inspired child." But all these
encomiums are fairly recent. For
most of his life, R. Buckminster Fuller
was known simply as a crackpot.

He is also something more. . . .
He is a throwback to the classic
American individualist, a mold
which produced Thomas Edison
and Thoreau—men with the fresh
eye that sees and questions
everything anew, and the crotchety
mind that refuses to believe there
is anything that cannot be done.

THELONIOUS MONK

by Boris Chaliapin
(1904–1979)

oil on canvas, 53.6 x 38.1 cm
(21⅛ x 15 in.)

TIME, February 28, 1964

Monk's lifework of 57 compositions
is a diabolical and witty self-portrait,
a string of stark snapshots of his
life in New York. Changing meters,
unique harmonies, and oddly
voiced chords create the effect of
a desperate conversation in some
other language, a fit of drunken
laughter, a shout from a park at
night. His melodies make mocking
twins of naiveté and cynicism, of
ridicule and fond memory. . . .
Monk himself plays with deliberate
incaution, attacking the piano as
if it were a carillon's keyboard or
a finely tuned set of 88 drums.
The array of sounds he divines
from his Baldwin grand are beyond
the reach of academic pianists;
he caresses a note with the tremble
of a bejeweled finger, then stomps
it into its grave with a crash of
elbow and forearm aimed with
astonishing accuracy at a chromatic
tone cluster an octave long.

JEANNE MOREAU

by Rufino Tamayo
(1899–1991)

charcoal, pencil, and
crayon on paper
72.4 x 57.2 cm
(28½ x 22½ in.)

TIME, March 5, 1965

Instead of the flamboyant, movie-star type [Rufino Tamayo] had envisaged, the artist found his subject "a most unglamorous girl of marvelous simplicity. From the beginning," he recalled of the sittings in his Cuernavaca weekend home, "she said we should talk in English because her mother was English and she preferred the maternal tongue. It was her own delightful way of telling me what I already knew—that my French is preposterous." . . . The Tamayo portrait . . . stirred mixed feelings in the subject. Said Jeanne: "I was struck by one thing when I saw the portrait [in progress], and that was the strength he found in me—not the strength I have, but the strength I would like to have."

RUDOLF NUREYEV

by Sidney Nolan
(1917–1992)

acrylic on board, 124.4 x 124.4 cm
(49 x 49 in.)

TIME, April 16, 1965

An Australian who now lives in London, [Sidney] Nolan is known for his brooding canvases, his translucent color, and his figures of man, often puzzled but always dignified. . . . He is a convinced Nureyev fan, has been observing the dancer since 1962. In London he once watched from the balcony for a week while Nureyev was rehearsing for *Romeo and Juliet,* a ballet that Nolan sees as "a ritual description of our civilization." The portrait depicts Nureyev in rehearsal costume, a kerchief round his head. "I wanted to show the feeling I got from him as he rehearsed Romeo," Nolan said. "He is a wonderfully perceptive artist, and I tried to get that in as well."

Robert Vickrey

GAMAL ABDEL NASSER

by Robert Vickrey
(born 1926)

tempera and ink on board,
44 x 32.5 cm
(17⁵⁄₁₆ x 12¹³⁄₁₆ in.)

TIME, March 29, 1963

PRESIDENT OF EGYPT

EISAKU SATO

by Kiyoshi Saito
(born 1907)

woodcut, 72.4 x 54.6 cm
(28½ x 21½ in.)

TIME, February 10, 1967

Today, the bold style and
clean line of Japan's foremost
woodcut artist [Kiyoshi Saito]
can be seen in major museums
the world over. . . . Saito was
an almost inevitable choice
[to portray Japan's premier],
but he approached the task
with some apprehension.
"After all," he said, "up to then
I had never done the likeness
of a face except of Buddhist
images and prehistoric
haniwa figurines." In one
furious sitting, the artist
squatted on the floor and
filled a large sketchbook
with his drawings. Back at
his studio, he transferred
a composite of his sketches
to five blocks—one for each
color—of a soft Japanese
wood called *sen*, from which
the cover portrait was made.

ROBERT LOWELL

by Sidney Nolan
(1917–1992)

watercolor and gouache on paper,
30.5 x 25.4 cm (12 x 10 in.)

TIME, June 2, 1967

"There's poetry all over the place,"
says Robert Lowell. "The world is
swimming with it. I think more
people write it, and there are
more ways to write it. It's almost
pointless—there's no money in
it—but a lot of them become
teachers, and a lot of them write
quite good poems and read to a
lot of people. Poets are a more
accepted part of society, and I
don't know if it's bad for us or
not, but it's pleasanter. . . . Still,
being good isn't any easier."

Robert Lowell, 50, is better
than good. As far as such a
judgment can ever be made of a
working, living artist, he is, by
rare critical consensus, the best
American poet of his generation.

The bulk of his best poetry is
seared with a fiery desperation,
fed by rage and self-laceration.
The world's ills become his own,
and his own the world's:

I hear
My ill-spirit
Sob in each blood cell,
As if my hand were at its
throat . . .
I myself am hell.

THE COMPUTER IN SOCIETY

by Boris Artzybasheff
(1899–1965)

tempera and pencil on Masonite,
53.3 x 40.6 cm (21 x 16 in.)

TIME, April 2, 1965

THE BEATLES

by Gerald Scarfe
(born 1936)

papier-mâché and cloth grouping,
approx. 120 x 130 x 100 cm
(47¼ x 51¼ x 39⅜ in.)

TIME, September 22, 1967

In case you weren't exactly sure, the way they are arranged on the cover, left to right, is George, Ringo, Paul, and John. This view of the Beatles is the work of Gerald Scarfe, 31, the British cartoonist/satirist whose grotesque caricatures in the British press . . . have been the nemesis of the high, mighty, and famous, from Lyndon Johnson to Queen Elizabeth. . . .

Scarfe started by sketching Ringo at the drummer's London suburban home, raced back to his Thames-side studio to construct a likeness on a wire frame with papier-mâché made of old newspapers soaked in paste. He followed the same process for all four. The figures are life-size head-and-torso, with paper-and-glue eyeballs inserted from the rear of the framework, hair made of scissors-fringed strips of the London *Daily Mail*, and a final facial of thin paste and watercolor. Each unclad figure took two days to build. . . .

Scarfe, who admires the creativity and force of the Beatles' music and is similarly admired by them, says that he "was trying to catch them as they are at present. They have moved on since *Sgt. Pepper*—the drug thing—to the meditation scene." Notable among the flowers, all of which are real, is the rose held by Paul, who told Scarfe that the Beatles' own guru, Maharishi Mahesh Yogi, once gave him a rose with this parable: "Here are the petals of the rose. Here is the stalk of the rose. But none of these is the real rose. The real rose is the sap." "And that," said Paul to Scarfe, "is what we are all looking for."

HUGH HEFNER

by Marisol
(born 1930)

polychromed wood,
185.4 x 76.2 x 198.1 cm
(73 x 30 x 78 in.)

TIME, March 3, 1967

Don Juan? Casanova? That was in another country and, besides, the guys are dead. Hugh Hefner is alive, American, modern, trustworthy, clean, respectful, and the country's leading impresario of spectator sex.

BOB HOPE

by Marisol
(born 1930)

polychromed wood,
48.2 x 38 x 40.6 cm
(19 x 15 x 16 in.)

TIME, December 22, 1967

They'd know that jaunty saunter anywhere. Bob Hope comes onstage with the cocky glide of a golfer who has just knocked off three birdies for a 68 and nailed Arnold Palmer to the clubhouse door. The crooked grin spreads wide, the clear brown eyes stay cool, and the audience roars its welcome; they can hardly wait for Hope to sock it to them. And so he does. Five, six gags a minute. Pertinent, impertinent, leering, perishing. . . . When he misses, the famous scooped snoot shoots defiantly skyward, the prognathous jaw drops in mock anguish, or he goes into a stop-action freeze. Sometimes he just repeats the line until the audience gets it. They have to laugh of course—but if they don't, it's almost treason.

LYNDON JOHNSON
Man of the Year

by Peter Hurd
(1904–1984)

tempera on paper,
55.2 x 37.5 cm
(21¾ x 14¾ in.)

TIME, January 1, 1965

PRESIDENT OF THE
UNITED STATES

L.B.J. AS LEAR
Man of the Year

by David Levine
(born 1926)

ink on board, 26.7 x 18.8 cm
(10½ x 7⅜ in.)

TIME, January 5, 1968

opposite:
LYNDON B. JOHNSON

by Pietro Annigoni
(1910–1988)

pastel on paper,
48.5 x 38.1 cm
(19⅛ x 15 in.)

TIME, April 12, 1968

P. Annig...m (H)
XV - X - LXVI

ROBERT KENNEDY

by Roy Lichtenstein
(1923–1997)

lithograph,
50.8 x 36.7 cm
(20 x 14⁷⁄₁₆ in.)

TIME, May 24, 1968

Pop artist Roy
Lichtenstein . . .
says that Kennedy
is one of the very
few real people
he has ever
portrayed. The
44-year-old artist
usually turns out
comic-strip-style
superheroes with
square jaws and
their girlfriends
with superperfect
coiffures. What he
liked most about
Kennedy, he says,
was his "lively,
upstart quality
and pop-heroic
proportions as
part of a legend."

THE GUN IN AMERICA

by Roy Lichtenstein
(1923–1997)

lithograph,
51 x 36.7 cm
(20¹⁄₈ x 14⁷⁄₁₆ in.)

TIME, June 21, 1968

TIME magazine,
New York City

COLONEL OJUKWU

by Jacob Lawrence
(born 1917)

tempera and watercolor on paper,
68 x 50.1 cm (26 13/16 x 19 3/4 in.)

TIME, August 23, 1968

LIEUTENANT COLONEL CHUKWUEMEKA
ODUMEGWU OJUKWU, MILITARY
LEADER OF THE SECESSIONIST STATE OF
BIAFRA IN NIGERIA'S CIVIL WAR

JOHN LINDSAY

by Romare Bearden
(1914–1988)

photo collage, 35.6 x 25.4 cm
(14 x 10 in.)

TIME, November 1, 1968

MAYOR OF NEW YORK CITY

RAQUEL WELCH

by Frank Gallo
(born 1933)

epoxy resin, 106 x 46.6 x 24.1 cm
(41¾ x 18⁵⁄₁₆ x 9½ in.)

TIME, November 28, 1969

The sculpture took three weeks to complete, and Gallo personally brought it from Champaign, Ill., to New York—it sat beside him wrapped in a first-class Ozark Air Lines seat. At first the package was too bulky to get the seat belt around, so Gallo was obliged to unwrap it. That caused quite a stir on the plane.

PRINCE CHARLES

by Peter Max
(born 1937)

cut paper and ink on board,
27.3 x 18.1 cm (10¾ x 7⅛ in.)

TIME, June 27, 1969

I didn't suddenly wake up in my pram one day and say "Yippee," you know. First I thought of being the proverbial engine driver or something. Then I wanted to grow up to be a sailor, as I had been on the yacht for the first time, and, of course, a soldier, because I had been watching the Changing of the Guard. . . .

Did ever a king speak thus? Probably not, but then these are exceptional times for once and future kings. The author of those wry and rueful words, lamenting a downward mobility forever out of his grasp, is . . . stuck in history . . . destined to become Charles III, the 41st sovereign of England since the Norman invasion.

JOHN WAYNE

by Harry Jackson
(born 1924)

polychromed bronze,
74 x 83.8 x 32.3 cm
(29⅛ x 33 x 12¾ in.)
(The work reproduced on the cover
was a painted wax sculpture.)

TIME, August 8, 1969

A Chicagoan, Jackson, 45,
followed Horace Greeley's advice
not once but many times. At the age
of 14, he ran away from home to
seek his fortune in a romantic
place called Cody, Wyoming.
There he learned the hard realities
of a cowpoke's life until World
War II and service in the U.S.
Marines (Purple Heart at Tarawa).
After the war and art studies in
Europe, he headed West again,
where he still spends part of each
year on a ranch near Lost Cabin,
Wyo. His brilliant paintings and
bronzes—of stampeding steers,
dust-churning ponies, and lean-
featured frontiersmen—have the
same quality of rough-chiseled
permanence that epitomizes
another kind of artist, John Wayne.

JESSE JACKSON

*by Jacob Lawrence
(born 1917)*

*tempera on board,
60.3 x 45.7 cm
(23¾ x 18 in.)*

TIME, April 6, 1970

CIVIL RIGHTS LEADER

KATE MILLET

*by Alice Neel
(1900–1984)*

*acrylic on canvas,
102.2 x 74.2 cm
(40⅜ x 29 3/16 in.)*

TIME, August 31, 1970

Until this year, . . . the [feminist] movement had no coherent theory to buttress its intuitive passions, no ideologue to provide chapter and verse for its assaults on patriarchy. Kate Millet, 35, a sometime sculptor and longtime brilliant misfit in a man's world, has filled the role through *Sexual Politics.*

 In a way, the book has made Millet the Mao Tse-tung of Women's Liberation. That is the sort of description she and her sisters despise, for the movement rejects the notion of leaders and heroines as creations of the media—and mimicry of the ways that men use to organize their world.

TED KENNEDY

*by Larry Rivers
(born 1923)*

*pencil and wood collage,
29.2 x 21.6 cm
(11½ x 8½ in.)*

TIME, November 29, 1971

UNITED STATES SENATOR
EDWARD KENNEDY

RICHARD NIXON
Man of the Year

by Stanley Glaubach
(1925–1973)

papier-mâché sculpture,
50.8 x 53.6 x 27.3 cm
(20 x 21⅛ x 10¾ in.)

TIME, January 3, 1972

WATERGATE BREAKS WIDE OPEN

by Jack Davis
(born 1926)

watercolor and ink on board,
53.3 x 48.5 cm (21 x 19⅛ in.)

TIME, April 30, 1973

RICHARD NIXON
HENRY KISSINGER
Men of the Year

*by Marisol
(born 1930)*

marble, 35.5 x 53.3 x 17.8 cm
(14 x 21 x 7 in.)

TIME, January 1, 1973

They constitute in many ways an odd couple, an improbable partnership. There is Nixon, 60, champion of Middle American virtues, a secretive, aloof, yet old-fashioned politician given to over-simplified rhetoric, who founded his career on gut-fighting anti-Communism but has become in his maturity a surprisingly flexible, even unpredictable statesman.

At his side is Kissinger, 49, a Bavarian-born Harvard professor of urbane and subtle intelligence, a creature of Cambridge and Georgetown who cherishes a never entirely convincing reputation as an international bon vivant and superstar. Yet together in their unique symbiosis—Nixon supplying power and will, Kissinger an intellectual framework and negotiating skills—they have been changing the shape of the world, accomplishing the most profound rearrangement of the earth's political powers since the beginning of the cold war.

NELSON ROCKEFELLER

by Marisol
(born 1930)

slate, 37.4 x 29.5 x 21.3 cm
(14¾ x 11⅝ x 8⅜ in.)

TIME, September 2, 1974

VICE PRESIDENT OF THE
UNITED STATES
Few men in American public life
have sought the presidency with
more fervor than Nelson Rockefeller.
"When you think of all I had," he
once explained, "what else was
there to aspire to?"

HENRY KISSINGER

by Philip Pearlstein
(born 1924)

oil on canvas,
91.3 x 66 cm (35¹⁵⁄₁₆ x 26 in.)

TIME, October 1, 1979

SECRETARY OF STATE TO PRESIDENTS
NIXON AND FORD
In office he always seemed to be at
center stage: the brilliant foreign
affairs analyst who never shrank
from controversy, the peripatetic
statesman who was forever soaring
off to distant capitals on secret
missions that, when revealed, sent
seismic shocks through chancelleries
around the world.

AYATULLAH
RUHOLLAH KHOMEINI
Man of the Year

by Brad Holland
(born 1944)

oil on canvas,
27.9 x 20.3 cm
(11 x 8 in.)

TIME, January 7, 1980

LEADER OF THE
IRANIAN REVOLUTION

JIMMY CARTER
Man of the Year

by James Wyeth
(born 1946)

watercolor on paper,
35.5 x 28 cm
(14 x 11 1/16 in.)

TIME, January 3, 1977

Just a year ago, he was walking up to men and women who did not know he existed, shaking their hands, and drawling, "I'm Jimmy Carter, and I'm going to be your next president." The political professionals were dead sure he did not have a chance—but none of the voters laughed in his face. He was such an engaging man—a trifle shy, for all his gall, and there was that sunburst of a smile that people would always remember. Right from the start, he was perceived as being a rather different kind of politician compared with the rest of the field—as different in philosophy and tactics . . . as in personal style. He not only knew what he wanted; he also sensed, at least in the primary elections, what the American people wanted.

The result was something of a political miracle.

JIMMY IN THE LIONS' DEN

by Edward Sorel
(born 1929)

watercolor and ink on paper,
50.8 x 38.1 cm (20 x 15 in.)

TIME, August 8, 1977

Having boldly jumped into the
world arena like a Daniel in the
lions' den, Carter is finding that
the inhabitants have quite a bite.
Soviet Communist Party boss
Leonid Brezhnev, deeply wounded
by the human rights crusade,
charges that Carter has launched
"psychological warfare," and
adds that "a normal development
of relations on such a basis is,
of course, unthinkable."
French president Valéry Giscard
d'Estaing says that Carter "has
compromised the process of
détente," while West German
chancellor Helmut Schmidt has
complained that Carter "acts like
a faith healer" and formulates
"policy from the pulpit."

MARGARET THATCHER

by David Suter
(born 1949)

crayon, pastel, and red felt-tip
marker on paper,
53.3 x 39.3 cm
(21 x 15½ in.)

TIME, February 16, 1981

PRIME MINISTER OF GREAT BRITAIN

RONALD REAGAN
Man of the Year

by Aaron Shikler
(born 1922)

essence of oil on paper,
66 x 45.5 cm (26 x 17⅞ in.)

TIME, January 5, 1981

If one were to take all of Reagan's qualities—the detachment, the self-knowledge, the great voice and good looks—and project them into the White House, he would have a first-class B-movie presidency. That is no insult. The best B movies, while not artistically exquisite, are often the ones that move us most because they move us directly, through straightforward characters, simple moral conflicts and idealized talk.

PAUL "BEAR" BRYANT

by Neil Leifer
(born 1943)

color photograph,
35.6 x 28 cm (14 x 11 in.)

TIME, September 29, 1980

To the rabid, almost reverential followers of his University of Alabama football teams, Paul William "Bear" Bryant is a nearly mythic figure, a man who embodies the traditional American values: dedication, hard work, honesty, and, above all, success. To the frustrated fans of the legions of teams he has defeated, he is a relentlessly slippery recruiter, a ruthless win-at-all-costs tyrant. To some, he is the demigod of the autumn religion, the finest coach of a uniquely American game. To others, he is the proselytizer of a brutal sport, a symbol of a national fixation on violence.

HOW JAPAN DOES IT

by Masami Teraoka
(born 1936)

watercolor on paper
32 x 23.5 cm
(12⅝ x 9¼ in.)

TIME, March 30, 1981

INDIRA GANDHI

by Mario Donizetti
(born 1932)

oil on board,
32.6 x 27.9 cm
(12 ⅞ x 11 in.)

TIME, November 12, 1984

PRIME MINISTER OF INDIA

It was typical of the proud, stubborn, courageous Indira Gandhi that she hated to wear a bulletproof vest and rarely agreed to do so. Certainly she was a fatalist. The night before her death, she had told a large, enthusiastic crowd in Orissa's capital city, Bhubaneswar, "I am not interested in a long life. I am not afraid of these things. I don't mind if my life goes in the service of this nation. If I die today, every drop of my blood will invigorate the nation."

For two days after her death, her body lay in state at the Teen Murti House, the great mansion that had been Jawaharlal Nehru's residence during his years in power, while hundreds of thousands of her countrymen came to pay their respects. Early Saturday afternoon, her body was carried seven miles in a gun carriage to the banks of the Yamuna River, an area where Mahatma Gandhi as well as her father and her younger son Sanjay had also been cremated. A million Indians had lined the streets to see the procession, and millions more watched on television as her body was placed on a flower-covered pyre of sandalwood and brick, and set afire by her son Rajiv.

LECH WALESA
Man of the Year

by Jim Dine
(born 1935)

*charcoal and pencil on paper
and photo montage,
25.7 x 36.1 cm (10⅛ x 14¼ in.)*

TIME, January 4, 1982

Anyone could read him at a glance. When things were going well, when it seemed for a while that the movement he led would brighten and liberate the lives of his fellow Poles, the face that grew so familiar in 1981 radiated delight: delight in his crusade, delight in his vision of the future, delight in being at the center of it all. In those moments, he held nothing back. But when things began to go wrong, when the tensions started to rise and the future he saw began to recede, the face grew heavy. The familiar walrus mustache sagged and the brown eyes turned weary. Again he held nothing back, and perhaps he could not if he tried. Lech Walesa is a man of emotion, not of logic or analysis. So was this movement, which he all but lost control of in the end, guided more by hope and passion than by rationality. That was the crusade's strength — and its weakness.

JOHN UPDIKE

by Alex Katz
(born 1927)

oil on canvas, 122.5 x 86.7 cm
(48¼ x 34⅛ in.)

TIME, October 18, 1982

"Among artists, a writer's
equipment is least out-of-reach—
the language we all more or less
use, a little patience at grammar
and spelling, the common
adventures of blundering mortals.
A painter must learn to paint; his
studio is redolent of alchemic
substances and physical force.
The musician's arcanum of
specialized knowledge and
personal dexterity is even more
intimidating, less accessible to the
untrained, and therefore somehow
less corruptible than the writer's
craft. Though some painters and
musicians go bad in the prime of
their lives, far fewer do, and few
so drastically, as writers. Our
trick is treacherously thin; our art
is so incorrigibly amateur that
novices constantly set the world of
letters on its ear, and the very
phrase 'professional writer' has a
grimy sound. Hilaire Belloc said
that the trouble with writing was
that it was never meant to be a
profession, it was meant to be a
hobby. An act of willful play."
—*John Updike*

RONALD REAGAN AND YURI ANDROPOV
Men of the Year

by Alfred Leslie
(born 1927)

oil on canvas, 152.4 x 137.2 cm (60 x 54 in.)

TIME, January 2, 1984

[T]here is a grave danger: if not of war tomorrow, then of a long period of angry immobility in superpower relations; of an escalating arms race bringing into U.S. and Soviet arsenals weapons ever more expensive and difficult to control; of rising tension that might make every world trouble spot a potential flash point for the clash both sides fear. The deterioration of U.S.–Soviet relations to that frozen impasse overshadowed all other events of 1983. In shaping plans for the future, every states-man in the world and very nearly every private citizen has to calculate what may come of the face-off between the countries whose leaders—one operating in full public view, the other as a mysterious presence hidden by illness—share the power to decide whether there will be any future at all. Those leaders, Presidents Ronald Wilson Reagan of the United States and Yuri Vladimirovich Andropov of the Union of Soviet Socialist Republics, are TIME's Men of the Year.

JESSE HELMS

by Alfred Leslie
(born 1927)

oil on canvas, 46.3 x 34.2 cm (18¼ x 13½ in.)

TIME, September 14, 1981

UNITED STATES SENATOR
One recent afternoon he was at home [in Raleigh, North Carolina], slouched in a living-room chair, feet in $7 mail-order sneakers flat on the floor. His dog Patches, essentially a beagle, quivered under the couch. Helms emptied his pockets—some change, a silver cross, a Christian medallion—and talked about his curious perch in American politics. "Some folks say I'm scary," he says. "The people here don't think I'm scary."

JOHN GOTTI

*by Andy Warhol
(1928–1987)*

*silkscreen on colored paper,
82.5 x 63.5 cm (32½ x 25 in.)*

TIME, September 29, 1986

HEAD OF THE GAMBINO CRIME
FAMILY, NEW YORK

MICHAEL JACKSON

*by Andy Warhol
(1928–1987)*

*oil and silkscreen on canvas,
76.1 x 66.1 cm
(29¹⁵/₁₆ x 26 ¹/₁₆ in.)*

TIME, March 19, 1984

Many observers find in the
ascendancy of Michael Jackson
the ultimate personification of
the androgynous rock star. His
high-flying tenor makes him
sound like the lead in some
funked-up boys choir, even as the
sexual dynamism irradiating from
the arch of his dancing body
challenges government standards
for a nuclear meltdown. His lithe
frame, five-fathom eyes, long
lashes might be threatening if
Jackson gave, even for a second,
the impression that he is obtainable.
But the audience's sense of his
sensuality becomes quite deliberately
tangled with the mirror image
of his life: the good boy, the
God-fearing Jehovah's Witness,
the adamant vegetarian, the
resolute non-indulger in smoke,
strong drink, or dope of any kind,
the impossibly insulated innocent.
Undeniably sexy. Absolutely safe.
Eroticism at arm's length.

VLADIMIR HOROWITZ

by R. B. Kitaj
(born 1932)

pastel on paper, 57.1 x 39 cm
(22½ x 15⅜ in.)

TIME, May 5, 1986

When he arrived in Moscow last week, a Soviet official asked to see some identification. "My face is my passport," replied Vladimir Horowitz, 81, returning to his homeland for the first time since he fled to the West 61 years ago. The pianist, who is to perform two concerts in Moscow and Leningrad under a new U.S.–Soviet cultural exchange . . . clearly retains a special place in the hearts of the Soviet people. A two-hour rehearsal in the Great Hall of Moscow's conservatory left 1,600 spectators cheering wildly.

DAVID BYRNE

by David Byrne
(born 1952)

photo collage, 40.6 x 30.3 cm
(16 x 11¹⁵⁄₁₆ in.)

TIME, October 27, 1986

LEAD SINGER AND SONGWRITER OF THE ROCK BAND TALKING HEADS, COMPOSER, AND DIRECTOR OF THE FILM *TRUE STORIES* (1986)

MIKHAIL GORBACHEV
Man of the Year

*by Nikolai Soloninkin
(born 1945)*

*papier-mâché box,
15.3 x 12.1 x 5.2 cm
(6 x 4¾ x 2¹/₁₆ in.)*

TIME, January 4, 1988

TIME magazine, New York City

Most readers may not recognize the style of painting employed for this week's Man of the Year cover portrait, but Mikhail Gorbachev and his fellow Soviets certainly will. The image is actually the top of a lacquered box. For more than 200 years, artisans in a handful of villages in northern Russia have been turning out such delicately painted artifacts. The boxes have attracted collectors around the world. . . .

Linda Jackson, wife of Moscow bureau chief James O. Jackson and a collector of the boxes, . . . journeyed 24 miles north of Moscow to the village of Fedoskino. There she found Nikolai Soloninkin, who holds the title of "merited artist" at the town's famous miniature-painting studio. Artisans of Fedoskino and the nearby village of Danilkovo are believed to have originated the genre, and their exquisitely rendered village scenes and portraiture remain unparalleled. Soloninkin, 42, spent ten days painting Gorbachev's likeness on a 4¾-in. by 6-in. papier-mâché box that had been slow baked in a 212 degrees F oven for nearly a month, and then covered with four coats of lacquer. The artist, who worked from stacks of news photographs, developed a rapport with his subject. "I really like the man," he says. "To me, he is much more an ordinary, down-to-earth person than some other leaders."

DENG XIAOPING
Man of the Year

*by Robert Rauschenberg
(born 1925)*

*photo collage,
49.5 x 35.5 cm
(19½ x 14 in.)*

TIME, January 6, 1986

LEADER OF CHINA

Deng's long career has been a biographer's dream, a tumultuous charge through war and revolution, exhilarating political triumphs and equally humiliating downfalls, personal achievements and family tragedies. Through it all, drawing on seemingly limitless reserves of energy and wily resilience, the tenacious 4-ft. 11-in. politician has managed not only to endure but to prevail. Today, one year into his ninth decade, he stands at the zenith of his power as leader of the world's most populous nation and as progenitor of what he proudly calls its "second revolution."

邓小平

I LOVE NEW YORK

by Roger Brown
(1941–1997)

oil on canvas, 127 x 96.5 cm
(50 x 38 in.)

TIME, September 17, 1990

TIME magazine,
New York City

WRAPPED GLOBE, 1988
Planet of the Year

by Christo
(born 1935)
photograph by
Gianfranco Gorgoni

plastic, polyethylene rope,
and globe,
45.1 cm (17¾ in.) diameter

TIME, January 2, 1989

TIME magazine,
New York City

This week's unorthodox choice of Endangered Earth as Planet of the Year, in lieu of the usual Man or Woman of the Year, had its origin in the scorching summer of 1988, when environmental disasters—droughts, floods, forest fires, polluted beaches—dominated the news.

While a team of writers and researchers worked on the stories back in New York City, art director Rudy Hoglund and deputy director Arthur Hochstein, who designed the layouts for the entire package, faced a difficult problem: how to create a strikingly original cover image. Their solution was to approach Christo, the famed Bulgarian-born environmental sculptor. In earlier works Christo had draped in plastic large sections of the earth—a stretch of Australian coast, a canyon in Colorado—but never the whole planet. This time Christo bundled a 16-in. globe in polyethylene and rag rope and drove more than 350 miles up and down New York's Long Island in search of the perfect combination of light, air, and sea for a photograph. The result—*Wrapped Globe 1988*—is a fitting symbol of earth's vulnerability to man's reckless ways.

ROBERT BORK

by William Coupon
(born 1952)

color photograph, 35.5 x 35.5 cm
(14 x 14 in.)

TIME, September 21, 1987

UNITED STATES SUPREME COURT
NOMINEE

JAY LENO

by Al Hirschfeld
(born 1903)
pen and ink on paper
66 x 50.8 cm (26 x 20 in.)

TIME, March 16, 1992

TIME magazine, New York City

If Carson was the King of Late Night, a slightly aloof and mischievous monarch, his heir, Jay Leno, the salesman's son from Andover, Massachusetts, is more like the Mayor of Midnight—a good-natured, sensible small-town mayor who knows everybody's name and believes in good government. To watch Leno win over an audience, to observe him shaking hands in airports, blithely signing autographs in coffee shops, chatting out his car window with other drivers, is to see a man engaged in a cheerful campaign for the office of Most Popular Regular Guy in America, a position he may already have won.

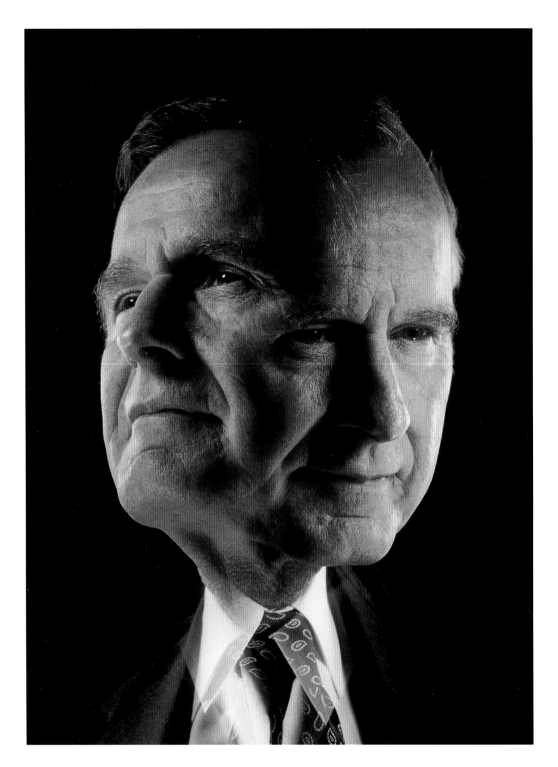

GEORGE BUSH
Man of the Year

by Gregory Heisler
(born 1954)

color photograph, 45.7 x 35.5 cm
(18 x 14 in.)

TIME, January 7, 1991

[George Bush] seemed almost to be two presidents [in 1990], turning to the world two faces that were not just different but also had few features in common. One was a foreign policy profile that was a study in resoluteness and mastery, the other a domestic visage just as strongly marked by wavering and confusion.

DAVID LYNCH

by Gregory Heisler
(born 1954)

color photograph, 45.7 x 36.8 cm
(18 x 14½ in.)

TIME, October 1, 1990

FILM AND TELEVISION DIRECTOR

WOMEN: THE ROAD AHEAD

by Susan Moore
(born 1953)

oil pastel, paint stick, and acrylic
on paper,
208.3 x 182.9 cm (82 x 72 in.)

TIME, special issue, fall 1990

TIME magazine, New York City

BILL CLINTON

by C. F. Payne
(born 1954)

watercolor, ink, acrylic, and
oil on board,
41.9 x 33 cm (16 ½ x 13 in.)

TIME, February 22, 1993

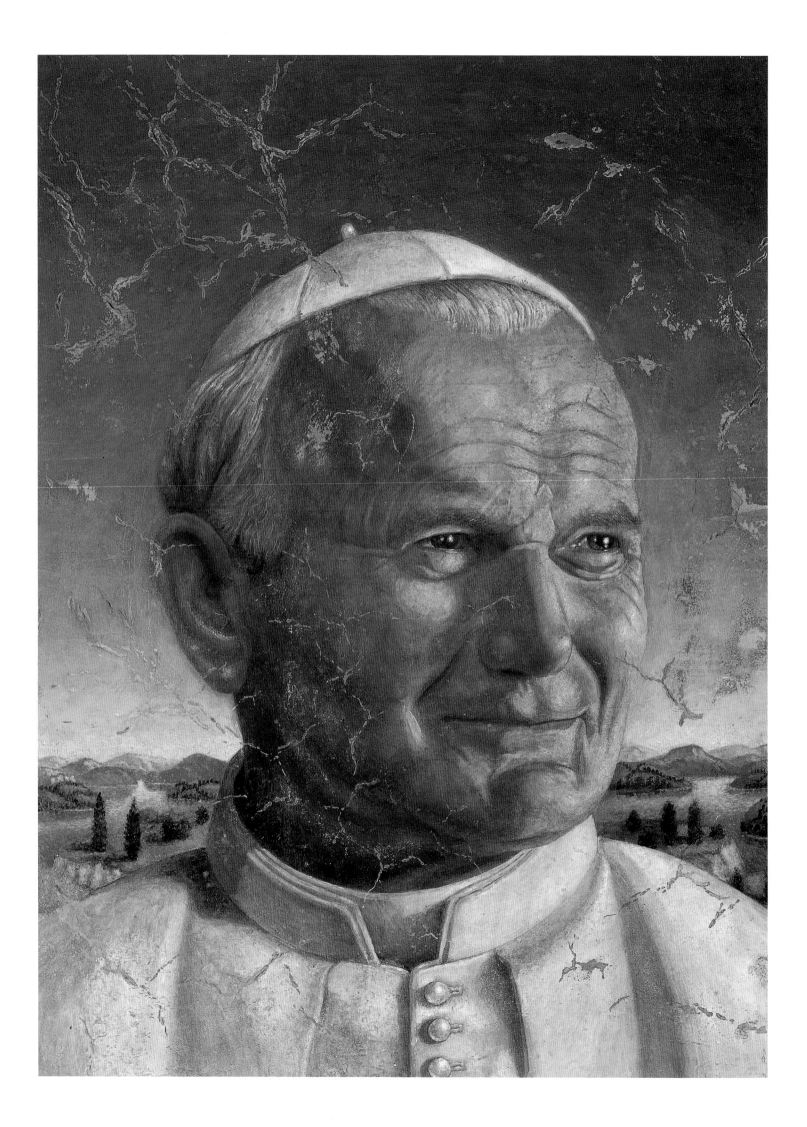

POPE JOHN PAUL II
Man of the Year

by Richard Selesnick and
Nicholas Kahn
(both born 1964)

fresco, 45.7 x 35.5 cm
(18¾ x 14 in.)

TIME, January 2, 1995

TIME magazine, New York City

CHECKLIST OF THE EXHIBITION

Unless otherwise noted, all items are owned by the National Portrait Gallery, Smithsonian Institution, Washington, D.C.; gift of TIME magazine.

Charles Lindbergh 1902–1974
Man of the Year
by Samuel J. Woolf (1880–1948)
charcoal on paper
TIME, January 2, 1928
National Portrait Gallery, Smithsonian Institution, Washington, D.C.; on loan from Germantown Friends School, Philadelphia, Pennsylvania

John L. Lewis 1880–1969
by Samuel J. Woolf (1880–1948)
charcoal on paper
TIME, October 2, 1933

Gertrude Stein 1874–1946
by George Platt Lynes (1907–1955)
gelatin silver print
TIME, September 11, 1933

Henry P'u Yi 1906–1967
by Jerry Farnsworth (1895–1982)
oil on board
TIME, March 5, 1934

General Sir Bernard Law Montgomery 1906–1967
by Boris Chaliapin (1904–1979)
gouache on board
TIME, February 1, 1943
National Portrait Gallery, Smithsonian Institution, Washington, D.C.; gift of Mrs. Boris Chalapin

Lieutenant General Jonathan Wainwright 1883–1953
by Ernest Hamlin Baker (1889–1975)
gouache on board
TIME, May 8, 1944
National Portrait Gallery, Smithsonian Institution, Washington, D.C.; purchased with funds from Rosemary Frankeberger

Admiral Osami Nagano 1880–1947
by Boris Artzybasheff (1899–1965)
gouache on board
TIME, February 15, 1943

Grand Admiral Karl Doenitz 1891–1981
by Boris Artzybasheff (1899–1965)
gouache on board
TIME, May 10, 1943

Marshal Tito 1892–1980
by Boris Chaliapin (1904–1979)
gouache on board
TIME, October 9, 1944
National Portrait Gallery, Smithsonian Institution, Washington, D.C.; gift of Mrs. Boris Chaliapin

Albert Einstein 1879–1955
by Ernest Hamlin Baker (1889–1975)
gouache on board
TIME, July 1, 1946

Winston Churchill 1874–1965
Man of the Half-Century
by Ernest Hamlin Baker (1889–1975)
gouache on board
TIME, January 2, 1950

Maria Callas 1923–1977
by Henry Koerner (1915–1991)
oil on canvas
TIME, October 29, 1956

William Hartack born 1932
by James Chapin (1887–1975)
oil on canvas
TIME, February 10, 1958

Charles De Gaulle 1890–1970
Man of the Year
by Bernard Buffet (born 1928)
oil on canvas
TIME, January 5, 1959

Dwight D. Eisenhower 1890–1969
by Andrew Wyeth (born 1917)
tempera and dry brush on paper
TIME, September 7, 1959
Los Angeles County Museum of Art, California; gift of Dwight D. Eisenhower (M.A.)

John F. Kennedy 1917–1963
Man of the Year
by Pietro Annigoni (1910–1988)
watercolor on paper
TIME, January 5, 1962

Pope John XXIII 1881–1963
by Pietro Annigoni (1910–1988)
charcoal on paper
TIME, October 5, 1962

Martin Luther King, Jr. 1929–1968
Man of the Year
by Robert Vickrey (born 1926)
tempera on paper
TIME, January 3, 1964

Buckminster Fuller 1895–1983
by Boris Artzybasheff (1899–1965)
tempera on board
TIME, January 10, 1964

Thelonious Monk 1917–1982
by Boris Chaliapin (1904–1979)
oil on canvas
TIME, February 28, 1964

Martin Luther King, Jr. 1929–1968
by Ben Shahn (1898–1969)
pen, ink, and wash on Japanese paper
TIME, March 19, 1965
Amon Carter Museum, Fort Worth, Texas

Jeanne Moreau born 1928
by Rufino Tamayo (1899–1991)
charcoal, pencil, and crayon on paper
TIME, March 5, 1965

Lyndon Johnson 1908–1973
Man of the Year
by Peter Hurd (1904–1984)
tempera on paper
TIME, January 1, 1965

Rudolf Nureyev 1938–1993
by Sidney Nolan (1917–1992)
acrylic on board
TIME, April 16, 1965

Gamal Abdel Nasser 1918–1970
by Robert Vickrey (born 1926)
tempera and ink on board
TIME, March 29, 1963

"The Computer in Society"
by Boris Artzybasheff (1899–1965)
tempera and pencil on Masonite
TIME, April 2, 1965

Eisaku Sato 1901–1975
by Kiyoshi Saito (born 1907)
woodcut
TIME, February 10, 1967

Hugh Hefner born 1926
by Marisol (born 1930)
polychromed wood
TIME, March 3, 1967

Robert Lowell 1917–1977
by Sidney Nolan (1917–1992)
watercolor and gouache on paper
TIME, June 2, 1967

The Beatles
George Harrison, born 1943;
Ringo Starr, born 1940;
Paul McCartney, born 1942;
John Lennon, 1940–1980
by Gerald Scarfe (born 1936)
papier-mâché and cloth grouping
TIME, September 22, 1967

Bob Hope born 1903
by Marisol (born 1930)
polychromed wood
TIME, December 22, 1967

"L. B. J. as Lear" 1908–1973
Man of the Year
by David Levine (born 1926)
ink on board
TIME, January 5, 1968

Lyndon B. Johnson 1908–1973
by Pietro Annigoni (1910–1988)
pastel on paper
TIME, April 12, 1968

Robert Kennedy 1925–1968
by Roy Lichtenstein (1923–1997)
lithograph
TIME, May 24, 1968

"The Gun in America"
by Roy Lichtenstein (1923–1997)
lithograph
TIME, June 21, 1968
TIME *magazine, New York City*

**Lieutenant Colonel Chukwuemeka
Odumegwu Ojukwu** born 1933
by Jacob Lawrence (born 1917)
tempera and watercolor on paper
TIME, August 23, 1968

John Lindsay born 1921
by Romare Bearden (1914–1988)
photo collage
TIME, November 1, 1968

Prince Charles born 1948
by Peter Max (born 1937)
cut paper and ink on board
TIME, June 27, 1969

John Wayne 1907–1979
by Harry Jackson (born 1924)
polychromed bronze
TIME, August 8, 1969

Raquel Welch born 1940
by Frank Gallo (born 1933)
epoxy resin
TIME, November 28, 1969

Jesse Jackson born 1941
by Jacob Lawrence (born 1917)
tempera on board
TIME, April 6, 1970

Kate Millet born 1934
by Alice Neel (1900–1984)
acrylic on canvas
TIME, August 31, 1970

Ted Kennedy born 1932
by Larry Rivers (born 1923)
pencil and wood collage
TIME, November 29, 1971

Richard Nixon 1913–1994
Man of the Year
by Stanley Glaubach (1925–1973)
papier-mâché sculpture
TIME, January 3, 1972

Richard Nixon 1913–1994
and Henry Kissinger born 1923
Men of the Year
by Marisol (born 1930)
marble
TIME, January 1, 1973

"Watergate Breaks Wide Open"
by Jack Davis (born 1926)
watercolor and ink on board
TIME, April 30, 1973

Nelson Rockefeller 1908–1979
by Marisol (born 1930)
slate
TIME, September 2, 1974

Jimmy Carter born 1924
Man of the Year
by James Wyeth (born 1946)
watercolor on paper
TIME, January 3, 1977

"Jimmy in the Lions' Den"
by Edward Sorel (born 1929)
watercolor and ink on paper
TIME, August 8, 1977

Henry Kissinger born 1923
by Philip Pearlstein (born 1924)
oil on canvas
TIME, October 1, 1979

Ayatullah Ruhollah Khomeini 1900–1989
Man of the Year
by Brad Holland (born 1944)
oil on canvas
TIME, January 7, 1980

Paul "Bear" Bryant 1913–1973
by Neil Leifer (born 1943)
color photograph
TIME, September 29, 1980

Ronald Reagan born 1911
Man of the Year
by Aaron Shikler (born 1922)
essence of oil on paper
TIME, January 5, 1981

Margaret Thatcher born 1925
by David Suter (born 1949)
crayon, pastel, and red felt-tip marker
on paper
TIME, February 16, 1981

"How Japan Does It"
by Masami Teraoka (born 1936)
watercolor on paper
TIME, March 30, 1981

Jesse Helms born 1921
by Alfred Leslie (born 1927)
oil on canvas
TIME, September 14, 1981

Lech Walesa born 1943
Man of the Year
by Jim Dine (born 1935)
charcoal and pencil on paper
and photomontage
TIME, January 4, 1982

John Updike born 1932
by Alex Katz (born 1927)
oil on canvas
TIME, October 18, 1982

Ronald Reagan born 1911
and Yuri Andropov 1914–1984
Men of the Year
by Alfred Leslie (born 1927)
oil on canvas
TIME, January 2, 1984

Michael Jackson born 1958
by Andy Warhol (1928–1987)
oil and silkscreen on canvas
TIME, March 19, 1984

Indira Gandhi 1917–1984
by Mario Donizetti (born 1932)
oil on board
TIME, November 12, 1984

Vladimir Horowitz 1904–1990
by R. B. Kitaj (born 1932)
pastel on paper
TIME, May 5, 1986

John Gotti born 1940
by Andy Warhol (1928–1987)
silkscreen on colored paper
TIME, September 29, 1986

David Byrne born 1952
self-portrait
photo collage
TIME, October 27, 1986

Deng Xiaoping 1904–1997
Man of the Year
by Robert Rauschenberg (born 1925)
photo collage
TIME, January 6, 1986

Robert Bork born 1927
by William Coupon (born 1952)
color photograph
TIME, September 21, 1987

Mikhail Gorbachev born 1931
Man of the Year
by Nikolai Soloninkin (born 1945)
papier-mâché box
TIME, January 4, 1988
TIME *magazine, New York City*

Wrapped Globe, 1988
Planet of the Year
by Christo (born 1935)
photograph by Gianfranco Gorgoni
plastic, polyethylene rope, and globe
TIME, January 2, 1989
TIME *magazine, New York City*

"I Love New York"
by Roger Brown (1941–1997)
oil on canvas
TIME, September 17, 1990
TIME *magazine, New York City*

David Lynch born 1947
by Gregory Heisler (born 1954)
color photograph
TIME, October 1, 1990

"Women: The Road Ahead"
by Susan Moore (born 1953)
oil pastel, paint stick, and acrylic on paper
TIME, special issue, fall 1990
TIME *magazine, New York City*

George Bush born 1924
Man of the Year
by Gregory Heisler (born 1954)
color photograph
TIME, January 7, 1991

Jay Leno born 1950
by Al Hirschfeld (born 1903)
pen and ink on paper
TIME, March 16, 1992
TIME *magazine, New York City*

Bill Clinton born 1946
by C. F. Payne (born 1954)
watercolor, ink, acrylic, and oil on board
TIME, February 22, 1993

Pope John Paul II born 1920
Man of the Year
by Richard Selesnick and
Nicholas Kahn (both born 1964)
fresco
TIME, January 2, 1995
TIME *magazine, New York City*

ASSOCIATIVE OBJECTS

Fund-raising prospectus:
"TIME /The Weekly News-Magazine/
(A Prospectus)"
Typescript, one page
TIME Inc. Archives, New York City

Circular soliciting subscriptions
TIME Inc. Archives, New York City

Henry Luce and Briton Hadden with
Cleveland City Manager William R.
Hopkins
Copy photograph
TIME Inc. Archives, New York City

Tear sheets of covers for:
Charles Lindbergh, *Man of the Year*,
 January 2, 1928
Adolf Hitler, *Man of the Year*,
 January 2, 1939
Computer, *Machine of the Year*,
 January 3, 1983
TIME magazine, New York City